A History of the Irish People

A History of the Irish People

▼

Presented In Ten Lectures

Dennis P. Sommers

Writers Club Press
San Jose New York Lincoln Shanghai

A History of the Irish People
Presented In Ten Lectures

Writers Club Press
an imprint of iUniverse, Inc.

For information address:
iUniverse, Inc.
5220 S. 16th St., Suite 200
Lincoln, NE 68512
www.iuniverse.com

ISBN: 0-595-20389-2

Printed in the United States of America

This Publication is dedicated to
Robert, Marie, and Jo Ann Sommers
Whose Undying Love and Support
Will Be Forever Cherished

Come away, O human child! To the waters and the wild
With a faery, hand in hand,
For the world's more full of weeping than you can understand.

—W. B. Yeats from "The Stolen Child"

Contents:

Introduction

People Study Irish History for different reasons, just as I'm sure all of you are reading this for your own particular reason. The fact is, today much of the world is studying Irish History. The profound influence this small island has had on civilization and today's world is only now beginning to be understood. The earliest inhabitants, who now date to at least circa 8000 B.C.E. (B.C.) apparently had an extensive knowledge of mathematics, natural phenomena, astronomy and the movement of celestial bodies.

The Celtic people, including the Milesians and the Gaels, whom we'll discuss somewhat in Lecture One, were the most dominant culture north of the Alps up until the first century B.C.E. and were masters of Poetry, Art, Religion, Spirituality, Military efficiency, and learning. In Ireland they remained dominant for another thousand years and contributed to Ireland's great scholarship, folk knowledge and lifestyle that was recorded and perpetuated by the monks through the monasteries and their extremely dedicated scholastic endeavors.

These monasteries retained and recorded this knowledge, history and, in fact Christianity itself, when the rest of Europe lost these to the barbarians and pagan tribes. They then reintroduced these throughout Europe, establishing monastic communities as the centers of learning, scholarship, public service, and spirituality, that were the dominant forces throughout the Middle Ages, establishing many institutions that are still with us today.

The ancient Irish Celts were probably best known for their sophistication and command of the spoken word, and later the written word. This incredible ability was probably what most fascinated the early Christian monks, and this survived nowhere more specifically than in Ireland. The literature and scholarship brought forth from the ancient Celtic bards and druids had by the seventh century stimulated intellectual activity in Europe that dominated the Dark Ages, and greatly influenced the all of Medieval Culture. It has dramatically influenced literature to the present day.

A great many of the world's most accomplished writers have come from Ireland, and most readily acknowledge their Celtic and Irish traditional influences. I've recently read that the novel "Ulysses" by James Joyce was voted by a Literary Society as the greatest novel ever written, and one can easily see the love of language, satire, and complex saga that Joyce employed and immediately attributed to his Irish-Gaelic influences. He was born in Dublin, as was Jonathan Swift, who 200 years earlier displayed the same qualities in "Gulliver's Travels". His biting satires of the inhuman English policies towards the Irish people spoke of the Celtic call for honor and equality, which have continued to echo through the ages ever since.

William Butler Yeats' masterful use of language has earned him the reputation among many scholars as being one of the top two writers ever in the English language. The W. B. Yeats Summer School, drawing faculty and lecturers from the world's most renowned academic institutions, is considered by many to be the finest literary gathering in Europe. Yeats also founded the Abbey Theatre, along with fellow authors Lady Gregory, and J. M. Synge. W. B. Yeats won the Nobel Prize for Literature in 1923. The Nobel Prize for Literature was awarded in 1925 to another Irishman, George Bernard Shaw, also born in Dublin; and, in 1969 to yet another Dubliner, Samuel Beckett. By the way all of these, with the exception of Shaw, attended Trinity College, Dublin, as did countless others of eminent stature, or perhaps more infamous, such as Bram Stoker, the author of "Dracula", whose mother told him tales of the cholera epidemics and the people who were thought to be dead only to later stir in their coffins. Dracula was originally titled "The Undead". In 1996, Seamus Heaney gave this small island the distinction of having the most Nobel Prize recipients of any country in history.

In addition to those just mentioned, there are scores of other famous Irish literary figures, the majority of whom were also Trinity educated men, such as Oliver Goldsmith, Edmund Burke (whose political philosophies formed the foundation of much of the American political system), George Farquhar, Thomas Moore, Oliver St. John Gogarty, Oscar Wilde, Standish O'Grady, Charles Lever, Sheridan Le Fanu, and others. There are a number of Irish-American authors of great accomplishment, such as Eugene O'Neill, who won the Nobel Prize for Literature in 1936, Henry James, and of course Margaret Mitchell, who readily acknowledged her Celtic roots by creating another Tara here in America, and developing a green-eyed Irish heroine who is one of the most dynamic ever. "Gone With the Wind" has sold over twenty-five million copies in half a century and still sells over 40,000 hard-back copies every year.

In addition to the Celtic, monastic and literary influences, we'll look at a variety of social, economic, and political influences, including Britain's role in Irish politics and culture as it has developed over the ages, and the ways in which these have influenced Irish life and society. We'll also look at modern Ireland and discuss the current events and people of both The Republic of Ireland and Northern Ireland as they attempt to implement the power-sharing provisions of the 1998 Belfast Agreement.

How did Ireland come to be called Ireland?

If you read of the earliest accounts of history it can be quite confusing. The island of Ireland is referred to by several different terms. The earliest writings–those basically prior to the Seventh Century —generally use the terms Scotia and Scot when referring to Ireland and the Irish People. These terms of course later came to be applied to current Scotland, which at that time was called Alba. The Greeks however, called the island Keltal (island of the Keltoi, or Celts). Hibernia (or Ivernia) was the Latin name used by the Romans and prevalent in the writings of Julius Caesar and others prior to the fall of the Roman Empire.

The name Scotia was derived from the name Scota. She was the mythical queen/mother of the Milesian people, who invaded the island around 1000 B.C.E. (B.C.) Approximately 300 C.E. (A.D.), during the time of Constantine, his poet, Egesippus, termed Ireland Scotia, and this term was used by continental writers more than any other for several hundred years. At the end of the Seventh Century the Irishman Adamnan referred to his home country as Scotia. As late as the Eleventh Century the famous Marianus Scotus (Marian the Scot) referred to the Irishmen as Scots. The Germanic author, Hermann, writing in the same century referred to them likewise as Scots.

Even in the Thirteenth Century, Caesar of Heisterbach, suggests people go to Scotia to visit St. Patrick's Purgatory, at that time, as it is yet today, a world-famous pilgrimage. St. Patrick's Purgatory is a cave in Loch Derg, County Donegal, where penitents once enclosed themselves for days or weeks in order to have visions of Heaven, Hell and Purgatory. Today they are usually three-day or one-week pilgrimages.

The modern name for Ireland most likely first originated with the Norsemen, or Vikings at the end of the Seventh Century. They referred to the Island by the name of Ir or Ire, and those on the continent slowly began referring to the island as Ireland. For several more centuries, however, the Irish scholars on the continent were called Scotus.

Adam De Breme, in the Eleventh Century, first promoted and popularized the term Ireland. The Term Scotland was then transferred to Alba because of the heavy colonization there by the Scots from the island, which began in the third century with the sons of Conaire the Great, King of Munster and High King of Ireland. They first settled the islands and coast of Argyle, as well as the northeast coast of County Antrim in Ireland, from where they initiated their crossings.

The Scotic (Irish) people eventually established dominance in what is now currently Scotland, as more and more came from Ireland to the aid of these first settlers helping to defend them against the aggressive attacks of the Picts. The chieftain Fergus brought an army from what is now County Kerry in the Fifth Century. The Picts were continuously driven north and northeast, until 850, when they were completely overthrown by the King of Argyle, Cinead (Kenneth) MacAlpin, who became the first Gaelic King of Scotland.

Now that the Scots gained dominance over the land, it began to be called Scotia, at first Scotia Minor (Ireland was Scotia Major), but eventually the term Scotia became associated with only Alba. In the eleventh century many of the Angle, or English people were pushed north in an attempt to flee the Norman Invasion. They settled southeastern Scotland, came into favor with the court at Edinburgh, and the Gaelic Chieftains were pushed to the highlands. The last Irish Royal lineage came to an end in 1287, when Alexander the Third died without an heir. This initiated the Wars of Succession between the lowland Old-English families and the Gaelic chieftains of the Highlands—Robert the Bruce, Wallis, and all that.

But, since the late Middle Ages, the island first known as Scotia has been called Ireland by most of the world. Other names associated with the island include Eire, which is the Irish-Gaelic word for Ireland and the official name as defined by the Irish Constitution of 1937. Erinn is the Old-English name for Ireland, with Erin being the modern poetic derivative.

Ancient Ireland

The history of Ireland indeed goes back to quite ancient times, and you can feel this often as you walk throughout the country. There are the ruins of many overlapping cultures, civilizations, and histories. The origins and nomenclature of the very oldest of these have been lost, but the spiritual presence of these long ago inhabitants can still be realized. If you allow yourself, you will often sense that you are walking among long-dead mystics, kings, poets, druids, saints, artisans, warriors and farmers.

The first people came to Ireland approximately 10,000 years ago. Before that time Ireland's climate had been too arctic in nature to support human life. Between 11,000 and 12,000 B.C.E., the retreating ice sheet left Ireland a scoured out island of little more than rock and bog. Around 10,000 B.C.E., wild horses and giant deer (larger than modern-day elk) crossed what was then a land bridge between Ireland and modern Scotland. They multiplied basically unchecked until the first hunters arrived in approximately 6800 B.C.E.

By this time water from the melting arctic ice had risen to cover the land bridge, but the level was over seventy feet less than it is today and the crossing from Scotland to Ireland was only a mile or so wide and was easily negotiated in small dugout canoes. The climate was continuously moderating and by now there were tall forests covering much of the island. There was still however dry land between Britain and Scandinavia, and it is speculated that these first Mesolithic peoples may have come from that region.

The first Irishmen were small dark primitive hunters and gatherers who ate fish, birds, roots, berries, herbs and whatever they could find and/or kill. They used stone and flint tools. They roamed Ireland virtually unmolested for over 3000 years before the first Neolithic ("New Stone Age") peoples arrived–around 3700 B.C.E., probably from Gaul (modern France), or from Cornwall and the Low Countries (the Netherlands). They cut clearings in the forests, domesticated the wild animals, built permanent structures, and began tilling the soil.

By this time the climate was quite mild and agreeable, similar to what it is like today. Except for approximately fifty miles of beach located on the east coast, Ireland is virtually rimmed by mountains. Ireland's climate is primarily the result of the north Atlantic drift current and the Gulf Stream current (the same current that goes up the east coast of Florida and America, and then travels across the north Atlantic Ocean). When these two meet, the cold and warm air vaporizes and produces a pure distilled mist or moisture over the island. This moisture gets trapped within the saucer-like interior formed by the mountains, and produces some of the most lush pastures and green vegetation to be found anywhere on earth. Hence, Ireland's famous forty shades of green.

The earliest archaeological evidence of these first permanent structures may be found at Ballynagilly in County Tyrone, and date to between 3700 and 3800 B.C.E. These early inhabitants used both rock and wood in construction (mostly oak, and from these earliest times there is evidence that oak trees were spiritually revered). These people were most famous however for the large stone monuments they constructed, called Dolmans, where they buried their dead and worshipped their gods. Some of the earliest of these are found in County Sligo, and on the high cliffs and in the fields overlooking Donegal Bay. These people also built large burial mounds, many of which can still be found all over Ireland. Some of the earliest and most elaborate (or at least well-preserved) of these are to be found in the Boyne River Valley in County Meath, namely at Nowth, Dowth, and Newgrange.

Newgrange, the most famous of these, is what is known as a "passage grave", with the cremated remains of its inhabitants being entombed at the ends of long tunnels, within a human-constructed mound consisting of thousands of tons of rock and earth. The tunnel at Newgrange is over sixty feet long and leads into a central area of three tombs shaped like a cross. At the entrances of these tunnels there are huge curbstones decorated with elaborate geometric designs, as are the rocks lining the insides of the passageways. The rocks lining the walls and ceilings of the tombs are even more ornamental with amazingly intricate patterns of circles, double-spirals, zigzags, herringbones, triangles and diamonds. It is believed that these designs held an astronomical importance, as all are aligned with the movements of the sun and stars, and on one day each year, that of the Winter Solstice, the sun's light enters the tombs for precisely one minute. These early people most assuredly intended that these tombs should stay sound and dry for all eternity, and they probably would have done so if it were not for the ravages of man.

Gold was discovered in the Wicklow Mountains around 2000 B.C.E. (the early Bronze Age—when the Minoans were constructing their magnificent Temple of Cnossus on Crete, and the Mycenaeans were settling mainland Greece). The ancient Irish began making beautiful gold ornaments and necklaces soon to be in great demand in the markets throughout Europe. This generated another, and the last prehistoric, invasion of Ireland which lasted from 2100 to approximately 1300 B.C.E.

The first of these people were known as the "Beaker Folk" (named for their style of pottery). They were a round-headed race from the great Indo-European family that developed into the various Celtic tribes. This was truly the beginning of Celtic Ireland, and these invaders developed into an extraordinarily tough, spirited, and mystical race of people. Most all present-day Europeans, Middle Easterners, and Indian peoples are descendents of the Celtic branch of this Indo-European family, according to most researchers. Their ancestors were the Ur people from the regions of the Volga Steppes in what is currently western Russia. They were among the first to domesticate the horse, and when they rode them into Thessaly around 3000 B.C.E., looking extremely terrifying and powerful, they gave rise to the legends of the Centaurs. They occupied Greece, Persia and parts of India until approximately 1750 B.C.E. They were also the founders of the Hittite Empire in Anatolia (modern-day Turkey and northern Syria), who became a great power from 1400 to 1200 B.C.E., and are mentioned in the Torah, and Old Testament Scriptures.

In reference to Ireland, the point of all this being is, that contrary to much current popular belief, the Celts were not a pure bloodline by any means. They were a blend of many peoples, some warriors, some traders, many were farmers, who intermarried and settled out together. They developed communities based on a common language, customs, occupations, religion, and identity. They assimilated more readily in Ireland with the native peoples than they did on the continent. Far more!

The use of iron, brought into westernmost Europe from the area of the Caucasus (between the Caspian and Black Seas), entered the culture of the Celts from between 1100 and 900 B.C.E. This made the Celts, who were already fierce and extremely feared warriors, even that much more devastating, and by the beginning of the Third Century B.C.E., they had become Europe's most dominant power–their power and sphere of influence extended from Italy, Portugal, and Spain in the South; to Rumania, Yugoslavia, and Bulgaria in the East; and, through most of what is now Germany, France, Switzerland, and the British Isles in the North and West.

This period of Celtic ascendancy is known as the "La Tene" period, named for one of the earliest archaeological sites found in Switzerland. This culture featured accomplishments that were far superior to anything known to date. In this hierarchical society, the aristocratic warriors shared the highest social positions with the Kings and the Druids, who were a combination priest, philosopher, historian, astronomer, teacher, judge, and poet. Artists and artisans were ranked only slightly lower. The particular Celtic peoples that migrated to Ireland were known as the Milesians and the Gaels, with the Gaels eventually gaining dominance over the island.

The Celts never much attempted to develop a written language. The Druids were the most knowledgeable and wished to only transmit their knowledge orally, to personally selected or chosen individuals. They could have easily recorded it as they were extremely literate, but chose not to, claiming it would lose much of its magic and power if this were done.

The Celtic peoples also constructed no temples–their religious rituals were performed outdoors in a grove of oak trees, which were considered sacred to the Celts. Their faith was also far more complex than anything yet known. They had moved from worshipping the objects of nature (the rocks, rivers, mountains, etc.) to worshipping the forces of nature (the sun, the sea, the moon, and the wind). This was extremely advanced at the time. After these deities they had a pantheon of lesser gods that governed every aspect of human life, such as fertility, agriculture, commerce, war, etc. These gods corresponded very closely to the pantheon of Greek, Roman (who pretty much copied the Greeks), and Norse gods. Remember–they all came from a common Indo-European ancestry.

The Celts believed the human spirit was immortal, they believed in reincarnation, and they believed that the human spirit could travel throughout life in a variety of forms. Music and poetry facilitated these travels and were practiced as being divine. Eloquence was as valued as bravery in battle, and a well-spoken poet could calm the most insanely enraged warrior. Diodorus Siculus, a first century Greek historian, wrote that when two armies faced off against one another, with weapons drawn and tempers at a fever's pitch, the poets would often throw themselves into the middle of the fracas and restore calm–as if they were taming savage beasts. Quite often, even among the most vicious barbarians, anger would submit to wisdom; and, the god of war would pay homage to that of the muses, and submit completely if the argument was articulate, truthful, and sound enough.

The art of the Celts was extremely elegant and sophisticated, and in great demand throughout the known world. They had learned enameling from the people of the east. They elaborately ornamented most all leather, wood, metal, and stone utensils, artifacts, and weaponry. They also learned the art of coloring glass, probably from the early Phoenicians. They were great weavers and dyers of fabric. They built the most ornamental, elegant, and swift of all chariots. They invented the bucket and barrel made from wood (usually oak), and these soon replaced pottery in northern Europe. They invented the scythe and rotary grain mill (two major agricultural advancements).

The Celts valued education as highly as fierce warfare, and one would study at the school of a Druid for more than twenty years to attain knowledge in philosophy, astronomy, law, religion, geography, history, and more. As previously mentioned, all teaching was oral and cast in verse, or poetic in nature, for easy memorization. These were the origins of the great Irish poetry tradition.

In spite of all this, the Celts were primarily known as extremely fierce and savage warriors. They were large people, with fair hair and skin, and were terrifying to the small dark people of southern Europe. Even more terrifying was their method of fighting, presenting a wild and furious onslaught of horsemen, chariots, and warriors. They would scream at the top of their lungs, this accompanied by the discordant blowing of horns, and the rhythmic beating of swords against their shields. Before going into battle they would dance wildly and leap around until worked into a frenzy, shouting insults and threats, and then many of them would rip off all their armor, helmets, and clothing, rushing into battle completely naked, and with no fear whatsoever.

After the battle they would engage in elaborate feasts where huge amounts of food, wine, and mead were consumed (mead was an alcoholic beverage made from fermented honey. It was also traditionally given to newlyweds and is the origin of the term "honeymoon"). Poets and bards would then tell of the warriors' exploits in the battles, as well as those of their ancestors. Another terrifying practice of the Celts was that of cutting off the heads of their defeated opponents, and then tying them to the necks of their horses. Later they would embalm them with cedar oil and display them on the walls of their homes.

Lucan, the Roman poet, wrote that death meant nothing to the Celts, as their spirits would immediately take another body, and even at times re-inhabit the same one. They were an outdoors people, understanding and worshipping all aspects of nature. They never built any towns. They never attempted to form a centralized working government or empire, although their numbers and sphere of influence were certainly vast enough to do so.

The Celts defeated the Romans and sacked Rome first in 390 B.C.E. (something the Romans never forgot). The great Roman legions of the era of Julius Caesar and Caesar Augustus held them in check for a couple of hundred years. Julius Caesar himself compiled a rather lengthy journal and wrote often about the Celts and Druids. He also dramatically reduced their numbers and drove them from Gaul in 51 B.C.E.

The Romans however, never got to Ireland (at least as soldiers—many came later to Ireland to study at the great monasteries), and the Celtic cul-ture remained intact there for over a thousand years with only relatively minor changes, until it was transformed into something of deep spiritual genius by the advent of Christianity.

The Irish Celts were in fact, as previously mentioned, a very spiritual and mystical people; and, there is a great resurgence of interest today among academics in the Celtic ways, and especially in the ways and activ-ities of the Druids, who, in addition to all the other functions previously mentioned, were also prophets and/or soothsayers (the Druids foretold the comings of both St. Patrick and St. Columba).

The Druids were also in charge of the annual festivals, which were based on the heavens and the agricultural cycle. There were four major festivals:

> Imbolc—the feast of renewal and purification celebrated on
> February 1. It was dedicated to the pagan
> Goddess Brigit, whom after the advent of
> Christianity sort of blended together with
> St. Brigit of Kildare.

Beltaine—a feast asking for a bountiful harvest and for good weather during the growing season. It was celebrated on May 1.

Lugnasad—the feast of fertility and first fruits. It was celebrated on August 1.

Samain—a festival dedicated to all the gods and the Celtic spirits of the "otherworld". It is the 3000 year old forerunner of our present-day Halloween. It commemorated the creation of the world and the transformation of chaos into order. On that night all supernatural entities, including the spirits of our ancestral dead, returned to wander among the living, thus imposing great danger as they hoped to avenge the wrongs that had been done to them. It was customary to put food outside the homes in an effort to appease the spirits who wanted to come back into the homes, eat by the family hearth, and then avenge the wrongs done them. It was celebrated on October 31, and was renamed "All Saints' Day", and then "All Hallows' Eve", following the advent of Christianity, before finally becoming "Halloween".

The Druids were mentioned by Aristotle in the Fourth Century B.C.E. and, as mentioned previously, were written about in the First Century B.C.E. by Julius Caesar, who wrote, "The Druids officiate at the worship of the gods, regulate public and private sacrifices, and give rulings on all religious questions. Large numbers of young men flock to them for instruction, and they are held in great honor by the people. They act as judges in practically all disputes, whether between tribes or between individuals". Cicero, the Roman historian also writing at the turn of the First/Second Centuries B.C.E. noted the Druids "had great knowledge of physics and astronomy"; and, the Roman historian, Pliny, wrote in the First Century C.E. (A.D.) that they were responsible for preserving medical knowledge. The extremely well preserved body of a 2000 year old Celt, found in a bog near Manchester, England, known to archaeology as "Lindow Man", is believed by many to be that of a Druid, primarily because of body markings, grave contents, and especially because of its unusually smooth hands.

There are two main theories regarding the origin of the word "Druid", both based on the ancient Indo-European language known as Sanskrit. The Sanskrit word for oak tree is "druh", and the Greek word for oak tree is "drus", and because the Druids revered the oak tree, it is deducted this is the origin of the word. The other theory simply goes one step further and combines the word "druh" with another Indo-European word "wid", which means "wisdom" or "to know".

As mentioned, the Celts of Ireland retained their culture far longer than their counterparts in continental Europe, many remnants remain in Ireland to this very day. The impetus for Celtic change, and the next major influence on the island, was Christianity. The Celts took to Christianity quite readily as they had long believed in persons of great faith and discipline being able to move back and forth from the human to the spiritual world. They also believed in the future coming of a great human god—a savior if you will. They also had no problem with angels, as they had long believed in spirits with similar responsibilities—through English translation and literary interpretation today these spirits are called faeries or even ghosts; but, when considering the original oral folklore tales and stories (as we know them) they sound just like angels. Many scholars have proposed that the early Celtic Spirituality was quite possibly the purest form of Christianity the world has yet known.

In Ireland, the period just prior to the coming of Christianity is known as the "Heroic Period". Our main source of information regarding the Heroic Period comes to us through a series of tales known as the "Ulster Cycle". The stories of the Ulster Cycle were perpetuated through the centuries orally by the Druids, poets and bards. These stories were then later written down by Christian Monks, who were extremely fascinated by the Celtic folktales and religious beliefs.

The stories deal with customs, great feats and journeys, love stories, kings and rulers, heroes, and of course wars (the tragic focus of far too many human stories). Here we first learn of King Conchobar of Ulster and his Red Branch Knights, who were ruthless and constantly at war with the rest of Ireland, especially Connacht, who was led by King Ailill and his fiercely combative Queen Maeve, who lived near what is presently Rathcroghan in County Roscommon. This was in the First Century—approximately 2000 years ago—rather interesting eh?

The most famous of the Ulster Cycle stories is an extremely lengthy epic poem entitled the "Tain Bo Cuailnge" (translated as the "Cattle Raid of Cooley") and relates the exploits of the great warrior hero Cuchulain (a beautiful statue of whom now graces the lobby of the General Post Office in Dublin). Cuchulain embodied all the cherished ideals of the Irish Celts—He was the Warrior/Aristocrat, full of courage, loyalty, truth, physical beauty, honor, deep respect for women, extreme arrogance, and a nonchalant disregard for death. He leaves no descendents (he kills his only son in a tragic duel). He is indestructible on the field of battle, an eternal youth, who is only conquered in the end by the deception of magic. No one now knows for certain how much of these tales are fact and how much is myth—but many of the major facts have been substantiated elsewhere—such as the names, locations and exploits of certain of the Celtic kings.

The kings ruled over "Tuaths", which were collections of families. A family was called a "fine" and legally consisted of all relation in the male line of descent for five generations. The Tuaths were the ruling forces in pagan Ireland. There were from 100 to 300 Tuaths in Ireland when Christianity arrived. The term "Tuath" also referred to the land each occupied.

The Tuaths were grouped into five over-kingdoms—Ulster, Connacht, Leinster, Munster, and Tara, each ruled by a High King called the "Ard-Ri".

The High Kings must be flawless—morally, socially, physically, and they were considered by the people to be descended from the gods.

Dagda (meaning the "good") was the main god of the Irish Celts (He was called "Sucellos" in Celtic Gaul). His son was "Ogma" (the "honey-mouthed"). He was the god of learning, and later, literature. Ogma's followers were the "filid" (the poets), and these went all the way back to the legendary beginning of Ireland, when Amergin, the Druid and son of Mil, chanted a poetic incantation to the beings of earth and sky, when he first came to the Irish shore. The Irish Celts had developed an alphabet and system of writing known as "Ogam" (after the god, Ogma), but it was difficult and cumbersome and was completely discarded with the arrival of Latin and the Roman alphabet, which made writing so much easier.

The sorcery of words was only equaled by the spell of music, which was bequeathed to the Irish Celts by the god, "Lug", who had received this gift from Dagda, who comforted his wife, Boann (namesake of the River Boyne), with music during childbirth. Music is of course still extremely important and mystical to the Irish. The national symbol is Dagda's Harp, and the Harper held the next most prestigious social position following that of Poet. (By the way, many of the oldest Irish settlements and inhabitants were located along the River Boyne, with their origins being uncertain–perhaps settlements of the gods?)

The Irish Celts also had a deeply sensuous respect for the ways and pleasures of nature, as well as a great fondness for animals. The horse was the Celtic passion and is still an Irish passion yet today. I don't believe that anywhere on earth does horse racing hold more status, and the annual Galway Races are the richest on earth, drawing competitors from every continent. (According to legend, Cuchulain's horse, the Gray of Macha, held him up during his final battle and supplied him with blood until they both died together.) The Irish Celts were renowned for their domestication of the great "Wolf-Dogs", which were in high demand throughout Europe and were presented to kings as presents.

When seven of them were brought to Rome during the Fourth Century, they terrified all who saw them.

The impact of this love of nature was at an all-time high during the era of Finn MacCumail and his son, Ossian the poet. His stories form the Ossianic (or Fenian) Cycle and came just after the Ulster Cycle, and the Heroic Age–the late second and third centuries. They talk of a deep ascetic love of nature–the song of a bird, the color of the morning sky, the falling of leaves, etc. Trees of the forest were protected by law and assigned various ranks, with the oak tree at the top and considered sacred. Finn's followers, the Fianna, lived solitary lives on the fringes of society, and surely laid the groundwork for the great Irish Monastic movement soon to follow. One of Finn's wives was a doe deer, and Finn could change into a deer whenever he so desired. The Irish Celts were extremely knowledgeable regarding natural herbs and medicinal botany. This they also passed along to the Irish monks, claiming they had received this information from the gods.

Other Celtic gods worth noting would include "Manannan", the god of the sea. He came from what is now known as the Isle of Man (named for him). He was a seaman who could look to the heavens and know whether the seas would be calm or stormy. Brigit, Anu, and Dana were goddesses of fertility and prosperity. Anu and Dana were the mothers of the gods, and Brigit watched over childbirth, bringing prosperity to the homes she visited, leaving her footprints in the ashes of the hearth. She was also the goddess of poetry. Maeve was the goddess of war and sovereignty. She was the namesake of the famous Connacht queen, but was worshipped in Ireland centuries before the Heroic Age. Every King of Tara married her symbolically. She was the Queen-Wolf who could outrun a horse, and her lover was Fergus, who ate seven times as much as any other man, had the strength of seven-hundred men; and, his nose, mouth, and penis were each seven fingers long. His scrotum was as large as a sack of flour, and when Maeve was away, he needed seven women. Welcome Christianity!

Christianity, Irish Saints and Monasticism

As we know, Christianity was heavily persecuted on the continent and elsewhere until the coming of the Roman Emperor Constantine, and his issuance of the Edict of Milan in 313 C.E. (A.D.), guaranteeing religious toleration for Christians. Earlier Roman Emperors saw Christianity as dangerously revolutionary and tried fervently to eradicate it. Christians were blamed for all natural disasters and military defeats because it was believed they angered the gods. Persecutions became most vicious under the Emperors Decius and Valerian in the third century but the last desperate, and surely the most ruthless effort, was attempted by Diocletian in 303, decreeing that Christians were not citizens and could not own property. He confiscated all Christian property, destroyed the churches, imprisoned the clergy, burned all sacred books, then enslaved and killed Christians by the hundreds (very similar to what the British would later do to the Irish Catholics).

Until the time of Constantine, Christianity was practiced in virtual secrecy, perpetuated mostly by the hermit ascetic monks living in the deserts of Egypt, Syria, and Judea. Under the influence of Constantine, Christianity flourished and spread like never before, and after the fall of Rome to the Christianized Alaric, the Visigoths, and the Ostrogoths in 453, the impetus for the growth of Christianity moved further north and west. This isolated ascetic monastic lifestyle was ideally suited to the ways of the Irish Celts.

A brief history lesson examining some of the early monastic movements may help to clarify this concept. Saint Antony of Egypt is considered to be the father of hermit monasticism. He was born in Alexandria around 250

C.E. Pachomius, a former general under Constantine, organized ascetic monks into the first structured communities, made them economically self sufficient, subjected them to certain rules; and, by the time of his death in 346, had established nine monasteries with over three-thousand monks, as well as the first monastery for women.

Saint Basil of Cappadocia (present-day central Turkey) then declared that monasteries should be of service to the community and established almshouses, schools, and hospitals at his monasteries; and, a rule (guidelines) for monasteries that became the model adhered to by most monasteries all through the Middle Ages, and is yet today the model for monasteries of the Greek and Slavonic churches.

The great organizer of western monasticism is considered to be Saint Benedict of Nursia (c.480-547), but by his time there were several monasteries already established in Ireland, as we shall see. Saint Benedict also wrote one of the early rules for monasteries entitled "The Little Rule for Beginners". In this he outlined specific organizational rules relevant to monastic life. In the rule of Saint Benedict, manual labor and prayer were the main focus, the Benedictine motto being "Ora et Labora" (a bit later on manual labor was defined to include academic labors as well). One extremely important new revolutionary concept expounded was that each monk must swear an oath of stability, uniting him forever to the particular monastery at which he took his vows (this became an extremely important concept for various monastic orders over the years). He also promoted that cenobitic (religious) life should be lived under the direction of an abbot at each monastery whose word was supreme; and, St. Benedict's rule exclusively. The abbots or founders of most the early Irish monasteries were Catholic Bishops.

Celtic (pagan) Ireland had no cities. The monasteries became the first "cities", and centers of education, spirituality, social life, and public welfare. In Ireland, all religious life was centered in, and revolved around, the monasteries—not the diocesan bishoprics and cathedrals, as was the case on the continent. (Note: It is quite possible that in many areas of the world yet today, as well as in the future, the monastic setting may again prove to be the most efficient and beneficial lifestyle, offering a superior education, compassionate and affordable health care, serious spiritual study, etc.)

Saint Benedict's rule was first brought to Britain in 597, by Saint Augustine, who had been sent by Pope Gregory I "The Great" (both were Benedictines) to both preach to, and of course convert, the Saxons who had just taken control of the island. Following the Synod of Whitby in 664 (called to settle differences between the Roman church and the Irish church), the Benedictine rule was the rule used by the vast majority of the monasteries in Britain up until 1540, when Henry VIII dissolved and looted all the monasteries.

I'm getting a bit ahead of the story here, we must go back to the fourth century and the influence of those first desert monastics, Saint Antony, Saint Pachomius, and Saint Basil. Disciples of these had moved into Wales, Cornwall, Gaul, and Italy by the end of the fourth century, establishing monasteries, schools, and almshouses in an attempt to Christianize the pagan Celts.

Two of the most notable of these, and the two who may have most arguably influenced Christianity the most in Ireland, were Ninnian and Martin of Tours. Both of these founded monasteries—Ninnian in the northern land of the Britons and Martin in Gaul (modern-day France). St. Martin of Tours was a maternal uncle of St. Patrick.

Many people mistakenly believe that St. Patrick first brought Christianity to Ireland, when he returned the second time in 432. There is substantial evidence to indicate that Christianity was known and practiced in Ireland by the end of the First Century. There are ancient writings that even claim the apostles James and Paul both visited Ireland in the First Century.

A Spanish Historian, Julian of Toledo, writing at the end of the First Century claims that St. James, addressed a letter from Ireland to the Spanish Jewish Community, and Vincentius of Bauvais stated that,

"James, the son of Zebedee, preached in Ireland, and when he returned to Jersusalem, where he was martyred, he had with him seven Irish disciples."

The writings of the Historians, Eusebius and Nichephorus, also claimed that these apostles visited Ireland and the western islands. They also wrote of several Irishmen, among them Conal Cearnach, who went to Jerusalem, were baptized, and took the faith back to Ireland and especially back to one, Conor MacNessa, probably a local king.

We know that the Roman Legions also brought Christianity to Britain from the First Century onward. At the Council of Arles in 314, we know there were Bishops from Britain in attendance. The Historian, Bollandus, writes that Palladius, who was sent by Rome to Ireland one year before Patrick and given the mission of converting the Irish, "probably found more Christians already there than he ever converted". He only stayed seven months, founded three churches quickly, none of which have any remaining evidence, and left. He did not get along with the Irish, and went to Alba (Scotland) where he founded a monastery and died only a few years later.

There is a good body of evidence that Irish Christians played a prominent role on the Continent well before the time of Patrick—several had gained considerable literary and ecclesiastical eminence. One of those most notable was named Manseutus (or Mansuey)—He was sent by Rome to be the Bishop of Toul (in Lorraine—the province of Gaul—currently on the border of France and Belgium) over a century before Patrick.

St. Florentinus, according to the historians was Irish. St. Florentinus was imprisoned at the hands of the Roman Emperor Claudius. While in prison he converted and baptized ninety-six people, including his jailer, Asterius.

The Christian poet Sedulius (in Irish, Siadal) was said to be Irish and was the first to translate into Latin much of the poetry and Irish rhyme, which up until that time was only found in Ireland. He traveled extensively throughout southern Europe and Asia, and dedicated one of his works to the Roman Emperor Theodosius.

The most infamous of all these was a brilliant rhetorician named Celestius, a famous lawyer in Rome, and disciple of Pelagius, who argued fervently his heretical doctrines about forty or fifty years before Patrick came to Ireland. St. Jerome wrote of him often, abusing him at every turn. He later went to Carthage and preached against St. Augustine of Hippo. He also argued before the Patriarch in Constantinople and the Pope in Rome, being forcibly ejected from both places. Dr. Douglas Hyde, writing in his "A Literary History of Ireland" also claimed that Pelagius himself was Irish, a belief several others also share.

Irish-Christian influence on the Continent has been well established, and Irish Historians are also in agreement that there were at least four of the Irish Saints active in Ireland before the arrival of Patrick—These were St. Declan of Ardmore, St. Ailbe of Emly, St. Ibar of Beg Erin, and St. Ciaran of Saighir and Ossory; and, we've already mentioned Palladius as well, who landed in County Wicklow, stayed only a short time, and then left (or was driven out by the Leinster Chieftain, Nathi)—there are various accounts.

I'll discuss a bit more about these Saints, but I don't wish in any way to diminish from the incredible impact of Patrick's coming to Ireland. It was an epoch of immense proportions, not only for Ireland but for the entire world as well.

Saint Declan was of the tribe, or clan, known as the Deisi, a very powerful Celtic people who had moved from the north to settle in Munster. He was descended from the Kings of Tara. As with all the Irish Saints, and Scholars, there are many stories associated with him and his exploits. It is said there was a ball of fire seen above the house when Declan was born, and as his mother lifted him up, his head struck a stone. Declan was not hurt, but the stone retained the image of his head, and when it rained, the water collected in this indented area, and this rain water would cure all sickness. As a young man, he exhibited neither faults nor ill desires. When he went to Rome to continue his studies, he was ordained a Bishop by the Pope and sent back to Ireland to preach and convert. Over fifty Romans returned with him, including Runan, the son of the King of Rome, with whom he was a close friend and whom he held quite dear. It is said that he also met Ailbe in Rome and they formed a close friendship that lasted all their lives. Another story claims that he met Patrick on the road as he was leaving Rome.

When Declan and his entourage reached the coast, they had no money and could find no boat to transport them. Declan had been given a little black bell by God for use only in emergencies. He rang the bell and an empty ship appeared with no sails. It carried them to Ireland and then vanished. The bell however was left behind. An extremely distressed Declan asked God for help and the entire rock upon which it was left floated across the sea and came to rest on the coast of County Waterford. The rock is still there with a hole in it, which was supposedly burned by the bell and, as the story goes, only people without sin can pass through the hole.

It is said that several priests and bishops have tried to have this object of superstition removed, but have never been able to find workmen that would perform this act of sacrilege, as the love of St. Declan remains that strong in the area yet today. Declan built his monastery and church where this rock came to rest and called the place Ardmore (meaning "Great Hill"). This land for the monastery and church had been given to Declan by the king of the Deisi. Declan was greatly loved as he founded several churches and according to legend converted more pagans than could be counted. When St. Ailbe was near death, he came and spent the last fourteen days of his life at Ardmore, where the two Saints engaged in peaceful contemplation and prayer.

It is also written that Declan visited St. David, the Patron Saint of Wales, who was also of the Deisi clan, but if this is accurate it would mean that Declan lived nearly two-hundred years. Declan was also reported to be present when St. Patrick converted King Aengus of Munster at Cashel, over a hundred years before David was even born.

Throughout history, Ardmore, which is located right on the coast, has at times been an island, and at times a part of the mainland. It is currently part of the mainland, but certain experts claim it will soon again become an island. There is a great round tower there and a stone cathedral, as well as a small stone house, where it is said Declan's remains are entombed. The northern Atlantic Ocean is quite wild and turbulent throughout this area, but it is remarkably calm and placid here at Ardmore.

As we've mentioned, Declan met Ailbe in Rome and they became life-time friends. Saint Ailbe is said to have lived 167 years, from 360 until 527. This may in fact be true, but it is more likely that this is a composite of he and perhaps one of his followers who possibly assumed the same name. Remember the accounts of these early Saints were not recorded until years later by the Christian Monks—and then only from the oral accounts passed down through the years.

Ailbe was born to a Maidservant in the House of Cronan, Lord of Eliach, in County Tipperary. Cronan was very upset by the birth of the illegitimate child and ordered that the baby be thrown to the dogs, wolves, and wild beasts so that he may be devoured. The Baby was protected by one of the wolves, guarding him and tending to him for three days until he was found by a Christian passing by. The Christian then took him away and raised him in the faith. Ailbe eventually studied in Rome, was ordained and sent back to Ireland by the Pope to preach and convert, along with at least twelve recently converted Irishmen.

They landed first in Northern Ireland where he converted the King, Fintan, and brought back to life three of Fintan's sons who had been killed in battle. He traveled throughout Ireland preaching until he finally settled out near his boyhood home at Emly, County Tipperary. There he built a church and school and wrote the "Rule of Ailbe", sup-posedly the first codification of ecclesiastical Rule in Ireland. He met Patrick at Cashel, which is just down the road, who reportedly named him Archbishop of Munster. He was greatly loved and adored, especially by Aengus, King of Munster whom Patrick converted. Ailbe supposedly wanted to go to Tyle (present-day Iceland) to retire and die, but Aengus wouldn't permit him to go because of his, and the people of Munster's, great love for Ailbe.

Relatively little is known of Saint Ibar—he was probably born in Ulster of royal lineage but the main focus of his activity was in County Wexford, where he built a monastery at Beg Erin, an island in Wexford Harbor (It is also no longer an island). Over 150 Monks lived at the Monastery and his school attracted scholars from all over Ireland and the Continent as well—most of these were probably Gaulish Scholars fleeing the invasion of the Huns—Ireland was already becoming a sanctuary for Scholars and Holy Men.

Saint Ciaran was born around 375 on Clear Island, County Cork. This is a rather small island in the southernmost part of Ireland. It was home to only a couple hundred people. When he was about seven years old, it is told he brought back to life a bird that had fallen from a tree. He was baptized at the age of thirty, still in a state of grace and then went to Rome to study. He returned to Ireland and founded a church at the present site of the city of Kilkenny, County Kilkenny. The Kilkenny area was at that time only inhabited by wild animals and Ciaran's first disciples were a fox, a wolf, a deer and a badger. A Wild Boar at first resisted Ciaran but then later returned to be tamed. It then cut the materials with its tusks to build Ciaran's first dwelling. He lived alone until the word of his holiness reached the people, and converts were attracted to what was probably Ireland's First Monastery.

These four set the stage for the arrival of Saint Patrick. It is very difficult to separate myth from fact regarding the life of Patrick, as the stories took on a life of there own over the centuries following his death; but, some things are known for certain. He was a Celt, and not originally Irish (for this reason he was not immediately embraced by some of these other Clerics we've just mentioned, especially Ibar) and the experts disagree as to the exact location of his birth. The theories range from the northernmost province of Celtic Briton, to the area that is now Wales, to the area of

Brittany (present-day France). In his Confessions, there is evidence to argue each of these.

More and more experts are of the belief that the Continental origin is correct, because it was from that region that he was taken captive at the age of sixteen. Also, St. Martin of Tours, previously mentioned, was his maternal uncle and lived relatively close to here. His father was a Decurion (Magistrate) in the Roman Administration, and was probably a Christian. Patrick was born c. 390.

Little is known about Patrick's early years, up until the time he was captured and taken hostage at the age of sixteen by an Irish raiding party under the direction of Niall of the Nine Hostages, King of Ulster. He was then sold to a farmer named Milcho and forced to herd cattle on an extremely remote mountain, Slemish Mountain in County Antrim. He was totally isolated there and lived on roots and herbs; and, stated in his "Confession" that he came to pray often, saying over 100 prayers per day. He also came to love Ireland.

Patrick learned the Irish language and was fascinated by the tales and fables of pagan Ireland. After six years of bondage, he one night had a vision that a ship was awaiting him on the coast. He escaped to the ship and after a year-and-a-half's travel, he finally made it back to his home. His family was overjoyed at his return and offered him land and livestock, but Patrick again had a vision in which he was handed letters from God charging him to become a priest and return to the pagan Irish. There was also a plea in one of the letters from the Irish begging him to return. He first went to Auxerre for study and was ordained priest and then went on to Rome where he was consecrated Bishop by Pope Celestine and commissioned to return to Ireland, the land he had come to deeply love. He returned to Ireland in 432, with twenty-four companions, some of these were Irish Christians.

There are many stories regarding Patrick's exploits in Ireland, and as we've mentioned it is extremely difficult to separate fact from myth, but there are a few things of which we're relatively certain, and these include the fact he evidently traveled over most of the island; and, his philosophy was to convert the kings, as he knew all others would immediately follow, and he apparently converted several kings–including Dichu, whom was the first, in County Down. There are several different stories regarding the method in which the conversions were accomplished. For example Dichu supposedly set the wolf dogs on Patrick whom immediately turned them into stone. Dichu then raised his sword to strike Patrick and was unable to move his arm. He was according to accounts instantly converted.

Patrick then proceeded down the Boyne River Valley heading for Tara, the seat of the High-King of Ireland, who at that time was Laoghaire, son of Niall of the Nine Hostages, the one who had originally taken Patrick captive. Patrick arrived at the Hill of Slane, just across the Boyne River valley from the Hill of Tara, on the night before Easter, which also happened to be the eve of Beltaine (the Celtic Festival of prayers, asking for a bountiful harvest and good weather).

The custom of the Celts was that on that night the Druids first lit a large fire to begin the prayers on the Hill of Tara. No other fires of any nature were to be lit before the Druids lit this fire. Well, Patrick lit a fire on the Hill of Slane, which immediately angered Laoghaire and the Druids, who then reminded Laoghaire that they had foretold this would happen, especially the most influential Druid, Matha Mac Umotr. He further reiterated that this was the fulfillment of that earlier prophetic vision and that the new fire lit would never be extinguished in Ireland.

Laoghaire then sent a party of warriors to either kill Patrick or bring him to Laoghaire early the next morning. Well, Patrick was already on the road to meet with Laoghaire, and had as we've mentioned learned the ways of the Celts. As he sensed the angry men approaching, he used the Druids own knowledge and when the warriors arrived they found only a herd of deer, with a fawn crying, and they passed right on by. It is said that Patrick then composed a hymn for God, called the Faed Fiada (The Deer's Cry) and he and his companions sang it on the road all the way to Tara.

Some scholars claim this is the first hymn ever written in Irish Gaelic, and yet today the Irish sing it for protection.

As Patrick entered Laoghaire's encampment, the king's famous poet Dubthach and the King's favorite nobleman, Erc, rose in respect for Patrick-the first two converts at Tara. He was then confronted by the Druids who tried to confuse him with their magic, but Patrick's miracles were greater than theirs, including dispelling the darkness, the one thing the Druids could never accomplish. Most present were then converted, including Laoghaire. Others say Laoghaire was not converted, but did allow Patrick to freely preach his faith.

There are numerous tales regarding Patrick's travels and preaching following Tara. It is known he traveled throughout County Meath and the province of Leinster, and then arrived in Connacht in 434. There he converted Laoghaire's two beautiful daughters, Ethni the Fair and Fedelm the Ruddy. He arrived at a place in County Mayo, now called Murrisk Abbey, as the season of Lent approached. It is at the foot of a steep mountain whose summit is in the clouds. Patrick decided to spend Lent high on the mountain fasting and praying in the extremely cold and windy conditions. He later said the entire time was spent in heavenly rapture. The mountain is now called Croagh Patrick and every year thousands make the pilgrimage to the top, most of them barefooted, as it is said Patrick was also.

As legend has it, before coming down Patrick ordered all the snakes and venomous creatures out of Ireland. The fact is, this tale was invented by Patrick's twelfth century biographer, Jocelyn, to add a sensational touch to the already huge mountain of impressive accomplishments attributed to Patrick. In truth, all the animals had been driven out during the ice age. When the glacial sheet receded, the rising waters covered the land bridges, first the one with Wales and a little later the one with Scotland before most of the animals could get back to Ireland, and after that none returned except those who could fly or swim. For over seven hundred years following Patrick's death this story regarding the snakes never existed.

It is believed Patrick next went to Munster where he converted King Aengus at the Rock of Cashel. He then convened a Synod of Ireland at Cashel, and summoned the four Saints of the South we mentioned earlier, Ailbe, Ibar, Declan, and Ciaran.

Following his work in Munster, Patrick again headed north towards Ulster, passing through Leinster where he and King Laoghaire agreed he should restructure and codify the existing Brehon Law Code, the new Code was called the Senchus Mor.

When he got to Ulster he founded the city of Armagh, built a monastery, a school, and a church. For the next several hundred years Armagh would be one of Europe's great centers of learning and religion. While at Armagh, Patrick wrote his "Confession" and "Epistle to Coroticus". Coroticus was a prince from Briton who made a raid into Ireland, killing and taking captive several hundred Irish—many of them Patrick's newly baptized converts. It's an intense document in which Patrick ironically condemns Briton's oppression, castigates Coroticus, and asks for the return of the hostages. The "Confession" was a defense written in response to having a dear friend turn on him and make false accusations about his life and character.

Patrick passed away at Saul in County Down, the site of his first church, around the year 460 or 461, leaving behind a terribly grief-stricken people. His final years were spent in prayer and contemplation. The twelve days of his wake are known in Irish as "Laithi na Caointe" (the days of Lamentation). Patrick's impact on western civilization over the next several hundred years, and in reality up until today could never be measured. It has been said that he is to the Celtic and European peoples, what Confucius is to the Orientals, Moses is to the Israelites, and Muhammad is to Islam.

Legend has it that when Patrick was near death, St. Brigit came to him with a beautiful burial shroud that she herself had woven. It has often been written that they were very close and had deeply loved each other ever since Brigit came to hear Patrick preach when she was young. His last benediction was for Brigit's nuns.

Christianity then took off in Ireland with fervent enthusiasm, for, as we've mentioned earlier, the new religion was quite similar to previous Celtic beliefs, and was embraced heartily by the Celtic peoples. The ascetic way of life was attractive to the Irish, and now with Patrick's work and encouragement, all elements were in place to produce a phenomenal Monastic setting, a distinctly Irish form of Christianity that would bring to Europe a new awakening and era of learning.

Saint Enda of Inishmore and the Aran Islands, Saint Brigit of Kildare (just mentioned), Saint Brendan the Navigator, and Saint Columba (Colmcille) of Iona were all dedicated followers of Patrick. They and their followers founded extremely influential monasteries throughout Ireland and the European continent.

Saint Enda, Saint Finian, Saint Brigit, and Saint Kevin:

We've been discussing several of the early Irish Saints (sometimes they're referred to as the Celtic or Irish-Celtic Saints). The terminology of "Saint" was used in pre-medieval times to denote clerics of great piety or purity. No Roman Catholic Saints were canonized until centuries later, and none of these early Irish Saints were canonized by Rome, not even St. Patrick. A bit later we'll discuss some of the differences that developed between Roman Catholicism and the early Celtic Christian Church.

Eighth century historians divided the Irish Saints into three distinct groups, the first being St. Patrick and the other clerics of the early Christian tradition whom we've just discussed. The second group included the founders of the great monasteries and centers of learning and the third group encompassed the deeply ascetic hermit monks who left the great monasteries and went off alone in the original Egyptian or Judean tradition.

Much of Ireland was still pagan at the time of Patrick's death, and many of the Druids began reclaiming their powers. The immediate followers of

Patrick were sincere, pious, and enthusiastic, but none of them had his great charisma or magnetism. The one to bridge the gap between the first and second groups, the one called the Father of Irish Monasticism, was St. Enda.

Enda studied at Candida Casa, St. Ninnian' School in Whithorn, which is located in western Scotland. When he returned to Ireland, he asked his brother-in-law, King Aengus of Munster, for the Aran Islands, off the coast of County Galway, for the purpose of building his church. King Aengus said he would prefer to have Enda remain and preach at Cashel. The elderly Saint Ailbe then spoke up in Enda's behalf and Enda made the ground rise up to show Aengus how fair and beautiful were the Aran Islands, as Aengus had never seen them and was afraid for Enda's safety. When King Aengus saw the beauty of the islands he immediately granted them to Enda.

Christianity had taken hold in Ireland with very little resistance and virtually no bloodshed—something that cannot be said for other regions. Because of this and the Irish Monks emphasis on scholarship and ascetic piety, Irish martyrdom is known as "White Martyrdom", as opposed to the "Red Martyrdom" associated with Rome, Jerusalem, and other areas of violent conversion.

Enda came to Inishmore, the largest of the Aran Islands around 480. The climate there is very mild as the islands are washed by the Gulf Stream. Flowers bloom year-around and occasionally you can even see rather scrawny palm trees growing there—from seeds possibly washed from Florida or the Caribbean. The climate is almost Mediterranean for three-quarters of the year, much milder than the Irish mainland.

The soil is extremely fertile but heavily rock-laden. The Rock Walls and structures covering the islands pay tribute to virtually thousands of man-hours of laborious effort. The monastery built by Enda became renowned throughout the all of Europe and both ascetics and scholars began coming in great numbers. Eventually, half the island was devoted to the monastery of Enda and the other half was devoted to ten satellite or daughter monasteries, each with its own Bishop or superior, but all under the direct authority of Enda until his death in 530.

Enda was very strict and a great educator. The Monks' days were divided into set periods of prayer, labor, and sacred study. They cleared and planted these rock-laden fields entirely by hand. They ate together in silence and their diet consisted of oats and barley, along with the fish they caught. They ate no flesh and drank no wine.

The fame of St. Enda's Monastery spread over the entire Christian world and most of his students came from the continent, whereto they would eventually return and spread the word of the Saints' sanctity and scholarship. It is said that over 120 Saints are buried in the cemetery there. It is true that the Roman Legions never invaded Ireland, but several came to Enda's Monastery to study, and at least seven are also buried in the cemetery there.

Among Enda's Irish disciples there were several that would carry on, and even surpass, the work that he had begun. Some of the most notable of these include Finian of Clonard, Ciaran of Clonmacnoise, Kevin of Glendalough, and the famed Brendan the Navigator, who came to Enda and prayed for the three days and three nights before beginning his voyage across the Western Seas to find the Land of Promise.

In 515, Finian established his monastery at Clonard on the banks of the Boyne River in County Meath. Finian was an excellent teacher and organizer, having studied under David, Gildas and Cadoc in Wales, as well as Enda. When he returned to Ireland he discovered that he was already known with followers awaiting his return, including the King of Leinster who had planted a great orchard of apples at the place Finian chose for the monastery. Nothing today remains of the Sixth Century Monastery, as unfortunately it was directly in the path of the Viking raids of the Ninth Century, The Anglo-Norman invasions of the Twelfth Century (led by Strongbow, the Earl of Pembroke and later by King Henry II himself), and then of course there was Oliver Cromwell who pretty much destroyed whatever was left in the Boyne Valley. At one point however, there were over three thousand monks living at Clonard.

From these, it must be understood there were hundreds of disciples, including those termed the "Twelve Apostles of Ireland", which included the extremely influential Columba (or Colmcille), in addition to the others we've mentioned. Finian was an ascetic in the tradition of the Egyptian Fathers, believing in simplicity, prayer, sacred scholarship, fasting, and labor that insured the self-sufficiency of the monastery. A part of every monk's day was usually spent in the scriptorium, mostly copying the rare vellum manuscripts onto parchment made from goat, sheep, or other hides. These parchments, the quill pens used, the natural pigments, and the carbon ink were all made by the scribes themselves. This was the beginning of the production of the world's oldest and most beautifully illuminated manuscripts.

Finian's School was open to everyone who wished to learn. Study was in Latin by this time, and consisted mostly of Biblical interpretations, with some time given to the Greek and Roman Classics, Virgil, Homer, Aristotle, Plato, Horace, Cicero, etc.

The presence of women in the monasteries was not shunned in Ireland as it was elsewhere. St. Patrick's entourage included several women and by the sixth century there were already a number of convents, the most famous of which was surely that of Ireland's female Patron Saint, Brigit of Kildare. She was born around 450 in County Louth, the daughter of a pagan chieftain, Dubhtach, and a female indentured servant. The King's wife was extremely jealous and made him sell the beautiful child. The sale of young Brigit was negotiated by a Druid, whom ultimately placed her into the home of one of his own Christian uncles.

All over Ireland Christian women were living with pagan relatives and Brigit decided to establish a monastery where these women could study and be at peace. She asked the King for the region known as the Curragh (today the center of Irish Horse Racing), and built her monastery on the edge of this vast grassland, near present-day Kildare. At first the king resisted but was then overcome by Brigit's incredible beauty and relented.

Brigit retained one very curious pagan rite, which is probably why today her legends are intermingled with the pagan goddess of the same name. She maintained a sacred fire out in front of her church. The flame burned day and night and was the responsibility always of twenty nuns. The fire burned for seven hundred years until it was extinguished by the Anglo Norman Archbishop Henry de Londres (Henry of London), in the year 1220. It was later rekindled and burned again until the dissolution of the monasteries by King Henry VIII in 1540.

Brigit's monastery, church and convent became models and were visited by many monks seeking directions for establishing their own, including Finian, and Brendan (whom we've already mentioned and will discuss in a bit more detail here in a moment). Brigit also traveled extensively founding numerous churches and convents, becoming a role model for thousands of Christian women.

One of those visiting Kildare was a shy gentle youth by the name of Kevin, whom Brigit took under her guidance, almost as a mother, giving him great counsel. He was born in 498, and lived to be 120 years of age, according to recorded accounts, however he may well have been a composite again of himself and one of his students assuming his name. By the age of twelve he displayed extreme piety, purity, and asceticism.

Wishing to retire from the world and lead a life of solitary contemplation, he ventured into the Wicklow Mountains. He there built a cell on bare rock, but it wasn't long before pilgrims sought him out, hearing of his great piety and purity. He then moved two more times before settling in the area called Glendalough (The Valley of Two Lakes), where he took up residence in a cave which was barely large enough for a man's body. This cave is known today as St. Kevin's Bed.

He prayed with all the animals of nature. Often birds perched on his head and shoulders, and it is said that one built a nest in his hand that he left undisturbed until the young were born and flew away. Animals brought him food and protected him day and night.

He was of course found again and his monastery-school that was established around these two lakes became a haven for students from everywhere in the western world, housing at one time over two thousand monks. Thousands of people yet today make annual pilgrimages to Glendalough, an extremely serene and spiritually peaceful valley. Little remains of Kevin's original monastery, but much was rebuilt from the time of his death up until the twelfth century, including an elaborately ornamented stone priory built in 1162 by St. Lawrence O'Toole (an Irish canonized Saint).

Another of St. Finian's Twelve Apostles was Ciaran, the founder of the Monastery at Clonmacnoise (meaning the fields of the hogs of Nos) on the River Shannon. He was born in 516 in County Roscommon and also studied under Enda at the Aran Islands, who was the one that directed him to build his church at Clonmacnoise. Ciaran lived only seven years after founding Clonmacnoise, dying in 549, at the age of thirty-three. Clonmacnoise however became, by the time of Charlemagne, one of the most illustrious schools of learning in the Christian world, a center of fabulous scholarship, art and literature.

At one point it was an elaborate Monastic City with at least 105 buildings, many of which were destroyed by the Anglo-Normans in 1179. The city was burned at least thirteen times, pillaged by the Vikings eight times, attacked by the feuding Irish themselves at least twenty-seven times, and pillaged by the agents of the dissolution, sent by King Henry VIII in 1553, who carried away everything including the window glass. In spite of all this, the remains today are still quite extensive considering, and stand as an ancient silent shrine to long-ago grandeur.

Many of the grand Sixth and Seventh Century Monasteries saw their greatest growth following the deaths of their founders. Their work was carried forward by a number of serious and scholarly followers, including St. Brendan, St. Columba, and St. Columbanus.

Saint Brendan the Navigator:

For some reason the Irish Monks always possessed something of a traveling spirit. Beginning with St. Patrick, they nearly all were compelled to travel and seek out new converts and build churches and monasteries in regions previously without the Christian influence. They all had a difficult time staying in one location, always curious and always trying to expand the boundaries.

Brendan the Navigator was born into a sea-faring family living on a peninsula stretching out into Tralee Bay, County Kerry, and always had the sea in his heart. He was born in 484 to a pagan family, and was fostered out by the age of two to St. Ida, who it is said remained in a state of perpetual martyrdom by letting stag beetles continually feed upon her body.

At the age of seven Brendan began study under the tutelage of Bishop Erc in Galway, who ordained him a priest at age sixteen. The king of Ardfert then granted him a plot of land in County Kerry, only five miles from his original home. There he founded a monastery with a small group of followers. It is also said that Bishop Erc instilled in him a tremendous fear of women, as all his life Brendan never associated with any women other than his sister, Brigit, in whose arms he would eventually die. Nothing remains today of this original monastery.

Since a very young age, he often perceived the need to be closer to God, always loved the sea, and believed the best avenue to redemption was to lead the life of an exile. There had been tales well before the time of Brendan about the land called "Tir na n'Og" —The land of youth and promise. (Following the advent of Christianity it was believed to be God's Garden of Eden on Earth). There is also evidence that the Irish Monks never believed that the earth was flat, but always knew it was a continuum. (Just one example of the many fears and superstitions that plagued Europe and kept people more ignorant all through the Middle Ages and beyond).

One night Brendan had a vision that he climbed a high mountain (now called Brendan Mountain on the Dingle Peninsula) and saw far out to sea a noble island with angels continuously rising from it. He then summoned all the monks to the monastery related this vision, and began preparing to set sail with those monks wishing to join him. They smeared rosin and pitch all over their very light, ox-hide boats, both inside and outside. Each of the boats was equipped with three rows of oars and sails made from animal hides. Each boat carried twenty monks and enough food and water for forty days.

They first went to Inishmore where they prayed for three days and received the blessing of Enda, before setting sail westward into the unknown. The voyagers kept journals and notes that were then compiled into a Tenth Century work entitled "Navigatio Sancti Brendani Abati". It was a great literary success and was studied extensively by Christopher Columbus prior to his voyage. He even came to Ireland to visit two monasteries and study the monks' original notes before he set sail.

These notes spoke of things thought unimaginable by the people of the day, such as huge pillars of incredibly beautiful light (icebergs which were west of Greenland and over halfway across the Atlantic and had never been recorded previously); and, Flaming Islands arising out of the sea (this spoke of the ever-occurring formation of the volcanic islands off the coast of Iceland, at that time called Thule–which is still occurring today). Up until the Sixteenth Century this region was considered to be the gateway to Hell. Brendan's Monks also first spoke of many fish the size of islands (whales), which travel in great numbers just off the North American coast. These and other phenomena have since been written about, documented and substantiated many times, first by the Norsemen and the Danes in the Ninth and Tenth Centuries, who also made the crossing to North America and also stated that Brendan had done this earlier (they had learned of this and other navigations from the Monks following their invasions of Ireland); and, later from a variety of seafaring traders from northern Europe and the region of the Mediterranean who ventured westward in the early Middle Ages. It is believed by most scholars that Brendan and his followers could never have known of such phenomenon if they had not in fact made the voyage

It must also be noted here that the "Navagatio" was a compilation of more than just the Irish Monks' seafaring adventures. It contained some rather fanciful and dramatic representations as well, such as the "Island of Man-eating Mice". When it was written the authors most likely embellished the stories somewhat to make the work more exciting, and perhaps marketable.

Brendan's voyage was probably possible due to the types of boats they employed. They were very light and very tight and rode across the waves like big baskets, even in the heaviest seas. In the sixth century this voyage would not have been considered nearly as miraculous as it is today. Many had sailed the seas in search of exile (the Irish Monks knew of the voyages of the Greek explorer, Pytheas of Marsailles, who in 300 B.C.E., discovered the "farthest islands" a full six days sail west of Briton). You must also remember that among these people there was virtually no fear. They were secure in their faith and miracles were expected. After seven years Brendan returned to Ireland and established several Monasteries in Connacht and Munster. He is also referred to as Brendan of Clonfert, after his best-known monastery, which was located in southeast Galway. Today there is a beautiful Twelfth-Century Stone church located there, highly ornamented in the Irish Romanesque style.

Brendan died in 577, age ninety-three, at the convent of Annaghdown in County Galway that he had built for his sister, Brigit. He was one of the great saintly Christian heroes for many centuries–all through the Middle Ages—and is still to this day considered remarkable for his achievements by all the scholars studying him. He was both the respected religious leader and the romantic adventurer.

Saint Colmcille (Columba) of Iona:

Another Saint extremely influential in spreading the Irish Monastic tradition of faith and scholarship was Saint Columba. He was born in 521, the great-grandson of Niall of the Nine Hostages, who first took Patrick captive. His baptismal name was Crimthann, which means wolf. Because of his great piety Crimthann was given the name Colmcille by many of his early friends, which when translated means "Dove of the Church"; and, throughout history he has become best known as Columba, which is the Latin version of Colmcille.

St. Columba first studied with Enda in the Aran Islands, and then under Finian at Clonard where he became one of the twelve Irish apostles. He became a great leader and an exceptional organizer. Following his ordination he returned to Donegal. His cousin who was the king gave him a beautiful hillside on the banks of the River Foyle, where the king himself often held court. The place was called Doire-Calgaich (the Oak-woods of Calgach) and today this hillside forms the original city of Derry, County Derry. Columba built his first monastery there in 546, building the church high on a hill in a beautiful stand of oak trees. Columba, like most of the Irish Monks loved to commune with nature and shared a special tenderness with the other creatures of nature.

St. Columba was a renowned poet and authority on the history of Ireland. Irish monastic education was much more liberal and varied than that on the continent. The pagan classics were studied in Ireland, and a special reverence was paid to the bards and poets, perpetuating their works in their own native languages. The rest of Europe for the most part studied only in Latin and the old languages were forgotten, lost, or at least unrecognizably mutated. Columba studied under a master poet by the name of Gemman who trained him in the old Druidic style.

At one point he returned to visit Finian and was shown a copy of the psalms that had just arrived from Rome. It was believed to be the first copy of the Vulgate (original Holy Bible, which was written or compiled by St. Jerome) that was ever seen in Ireland. Finian treasured the great manuscript and allowed Columba to read it, but had forbidden him to copy it. Well, Columba stayed up all night a few nights and secretly copied it. When this was discovered, Finian demanded the copy as well as the original. Columba refused to render the copy and the matter was taken before the High King at Tara, Diarmait. Diarmait ruled in Finian's favor. A short time later during a game of hurling, a son of the King of Connacht accidentally killed one of Diarmait's sons. He ran to the sanctuary of Columba's church for protection, where Diarmait's soldiers defiled the church by breaking in and seizing the man. This infuriated Columba.

Columba encouraged an army to be organized and march against Diarmait. The two armies met at Culdreimhne in County Sligo and over three thousand men were killed. This ultimately led to the fall of Diarmait and that of Tara itself. The victorious army wished to place Columba on the throne as the High King of Ireland, but Columba refused the position, being extremely remorseful. His self-reproach was exceptionally severe and he concluded that his only restitution could be to convert as many souls as had perished due to his actions. He decided on self-imposed exile and chose the land of modern-day Scotland, which was called Alba or Pictland at that time. Scotland was during that period mainly ruled by the Picts (basically a combination of Celtic People and an earlier Neolithic race).

Columba left Ireland in 563, accompanied by twelve clerics. (This became traditional with the Irish monks, following in the pattern of Christ.) They first made landfall in Alba at a place called Kintyre, but soon decided to move on and landed at the island of Iona, about one mile off the large island of Mull, and approximately seventy-five miles from Ireland. The earth here is more fertile than one would suspect due to the high concentration of lime in the shell sand, and the waters are full of fish and seals, a plentiful supply of meat, hides, and burnable oil. St. Columba built his monastery on a high hill overlooking the eastern coast.

Columba's Rule was strict and he also placed a great emphasis on the work of the scribes in the scriptorium. In 806, when the Norse raided Iona and killed eighty-six of the Monks, the survivors went back to Ireland and founded the Monastery at Kells that produced the great illuminated manuscript (a copy of the gospels). The followers of Columba created some of the most beautiful illuminated manuscripts the world has ever known, including also the Book of Durrow (both of these, along with the Book of Armagh and others are currently housed in the library at Trinity College, Dublin).

Iona was situated directly on the edge of the lands controlled by the pagan picts, and Columba knew the monastery's survival depended on his gaining the favor of the pagan king, Brude (I'm sure following the style of Patrick). Columba went to Inverness, the Pict's capital, but Brude barred the gates on the advice of his Druid, Broichan. According to legend, Columba made the sign of the cross and the gates flew open. Columba was then received with great respect by the king, and from that day forward Brude admired, honored and supported this holy man. They spoke often in an atmosphere of peace and a new awakening came to the land of the Picts. The Irish Monks brought great knowledge to the Picts in addition to the Christian faith, including advanced agricultural practices, knowledge of medicine and medicinal herbs, and their first educational system.

Columba's monks traveled throughout Alba and the Highlands, preaching and teaching. One of his disciples, Cormac, sailed around the northern tip of Scotland, sailed across the extremely dangerous passage between the Atlantic and the North Sea, and settled on Orkney Island where he established a monastery and preached to the Picts. He also sailed as far as the Faeroe Islands, Iceland and Greenland. Cormac eventually ended up back at Iona, but Columba told him his work was in Durrow and sent him there.

Columba was primarily responsible for the Christianizing of Scotland and in 574, Aidan, the grandson of Fergus, became the first Christian King of Scotland. He and Columba formed an alliance, which was cultural and political, as well as religious. This ultimately led to an alliance between Christian Ireland and Christian Scotland that would endure for centuries, sharing Saints and Scholarship; and, uniting against the invasions of the Saxons, Vikings and Danes.

In 597, thirty-four years after Columba came to Iona, Rome and Pope Gregory I sent the papal emissary Augustine to convert the Saxons and Britons. He became the first Bishop of Canterbury, but was not well received by any but the Saxons. Approximately 604, a follower of Columba, Aidan of Iona, was instructed by King Oswald of Northumbria, to establish a monastery at Lindisfarne, which for the next thirty years became the stronghold of Christian scholarship in northern Briton. It was inevitable that the two great Christian traditions, that of Rome and that of the Irish, were about to clash.

The Irish church had never been directly under the control, nor particularly obedient, to Rome–subservience was not really an Irish trait. The Irish ways were considered suspect by Rome, who was basically power-orientated, creating also a great political and economic machine. The Irish asceticism, love of nature, and emphasis on truth did not necessarily fit into this machine. The Romans had created a new calendar and recalculated the date of Easter to fit into this calendar. This Irish still celebrated Easter according to the original calculations. There were also a number of liturgical and organizational questions on which the two churches differed.

Tensions mounted and in 664, the King of Northumbria, Oswy, called a synod at the monastery founded by Hilda at Whitby, to settle the arguments. At the Synod of Whitby, Bishop Colman, Abbot of Lindisfarne, presented the Irish position, with the English and/or Roman position being delivered by Wilfred, the Abbot of Ripon Monastery. Wilfred was shrewd, prepared for argument, and claimed the whole world outside of these islands was on the side of Rome. Colman had not really planned nor prepared, relying on his eloquence and the absolute correctness or truth of his position. The deciding blow was struck when Wilfred quoted Jesus as saying, "Thou art Peter, and upon this rock I will build my church, and the gates of hell shall not prevail against it, and to thee I will give the keys of my kingdom in heaven." (Rome of course had always claimed that Peter founded the church there, was the first Bishop of Rome, and is even buried beneath St. Peter's Basilica). Basically, King Oswy was afraid to rule against this argument and ruled in favor of Wilfred.

In defeat, Bishop Colman took the Irish monks from Lindisfarne, went to Iona, and then on to Galway where he founded a monastery on the island of Inishbofin. Lindisfarne has the dubious distinction of then becoming the first monastery raided and destroyed by the Vikings in 793. It was however, revived by the Normans in the Eleventh Century and is today something of a Riviera-like tourist attraction.

As you can see, a great deal of historical influence can be attributed to Saint Columba. He died in 597, after a series of Norse raids beginning in 595.

His remains were taken to Dunkeld in the Scottish Highlands, and then eventually removed to Downpatrick, where they are entombed with those of St. Patrick and St. Brigit.

Saint Columbanus of Luxeuil:

I'd like to briefly discuss one more of the great traveling Irish Saints. He is St. Columbanus of Luxeuil, the founder of monasteries from Briton, through Gaul, and into Italy, Germany and Switzerland. He was born in 543, in Leinster. His mother had a vision before he was born in which she saw the sun rising from her bosom to light up the world. She took exceptional care of Columbanus who came to be known as the "Child of Light". Most of his life he would seek out desolate places where he could pray and commune with the forests and the wild animals of nature.

He first studied at a monastery located at Lough Erne in County Fermanagh, where the Abbot was Sinell, a disciple of Finian's. There he learned the Scriptures well and wrote sacred poetry. Sinell then recommended him for Comgall's excellent school located at Bangor, where many of the finest minds of the age were then gathered. He must have liked the atmosphere because he stayed there approximately thirty years, attaining the position of Principal Teacher. He was much loved by everyone and valued most highly by Comgall.

At forty-eight years of age the urge again came to him to seek contemplative exile. He had learned a great deal, both scholastically or academically, and regarding the workings of a monastery. In 591 he landed on the coast of Breton, and made his way south into Burgundy–at that time within the kingdom of the Merovingians and inhabited by the Franks. The King of the Franks at that time was Childebert II, great-grandson of Clovis I, founder of the Merovingian dynasty, but the real power was held by Childebert's mother Queen Brunhilda.

The king asked Columbanus to preach a sermon in Latin and was so moved by it that he asked the monk to stay there. He was given land in a region which is today located on the border between Switzerland and Germany. It was the location of an old Roman fort called Anegrates (today Annegray) and the monks rebuilt the walls of the old fort, as well as what had been a temple to the goddess Diana, which was rededicated to the patron saint of the region St. Martin of Tours (Patrick's uncle). The life there was extremely tough. Europe, and especially this region, was very combative–far more so than Ireland. There were constantly raids perpetuated by the violent warlords.

The monks had nothing worth taking except food and the monks were often on the verge of starvation. They were very near death at one point when all of a sudden a man showed up with two large horses laden with food. Quite some time earlier this man's wife had been near death and the monks prayed for her and she recovered. The man wanted to show his appreciation. After this event many of the region's inhabitants began bringing their illnesses to the monastery and soon hundreds were flocking to the monastery to be healed. They were fascinated by the mysticism of the spiritual message and the peaceful, passive nature of the monks, both concepts quite foreign to a people with only an aggressive, pagan, and violent history.

Columbanus has always been revered throughout this region. In 1945, the sculptor Claude Granges erected a large bronze of Columbanus that stands outside the current Thirteenth Century Church in the city of Luxeuil, which is today still a major health resort and center of healing.

We all know how politics seems to have destroyed many good things over the centuries, well this also happened at Luxeuil. Warring for lands and kingdoms was the way of life in this region and two of Brunhilda's sons wanted these particular lands. Brunhilda wanted Columbanus to baptize two illegitimate heirs and when Columbanus refused, the monks were expelled from Luxeuil and Annegray in 610.

They were going to make their way back to Ireland, but literally missed the boat, and wandered back across France (or Gaul), and eventually ended up on a boat heading up the Rhine River to Lake Constance. They arrived there in 612. In 613, Columbanus and his monks headed out across the Alps, an incredibly cold and dangerous journey, but they eventually reached the Plain of Lombardy, ruled by Duke Agilulf, who held court and resided in Milan. He liked the courageous monks and asked them to stay.

Columbanus founded his final monastery at a place called Bobbio, where the River Bobbio met another mountain stream and formed a beautiful valley. After the death of Brunhilda, the Frankish King Lothar II asked Columbanus to return to Luxeuil, but he refused, as he had become heavily involved in the Arian Heresy in Italy. In 615, he retired to a cave alone high in the mountains where he died in the company of the animals he loved. He is buried in a beautiful marble tomb located at the picturesque stone church in Bobbio. Columbanus had brought great faith and scholarship throughout a vast region of violent and pagan warlords.

Saints like Columba and Columbanus were men of profound faith and spirituality, but they were also exceptional scholars and organizers. Each monastery was a self-sufficient entity ruled by an Abbot—something of a small town if you will; and, in Ireland as was mentioned earlier, these were basically the only towns and most definitely the largest settlements. Hence, they became the first targets of the Norse raids and invasions, which began in the late Eighth Century.

The Viking and Norman Invasions

The Norse and the Danes:

The period of the Vikings, which began in the Eighth Century, lasted almost four hundred years. The first Vikings to come to Ireland were the Norsemen from the areas of Norway and Sweden. Their homelands were becoming over-populated, the lands were not particularly fertile, and economic crisis was setting in. They set out looking for more fertile lands in a more favorable climate. They were basically an adventurous, warring, and pagan people.

They had first gone to Iceland where they encountered the settlements of the Irish Monks and learned of the warm fertile lands located just a bit further south. The first Irish contact with the Norsemen came in 794 or 795, there are varying accounts, when they attacked and devastated the Island of Rechru (currently Lambay) just off Howth, slightly north of Dublin. They sacked the monastery there that had been one of the first founded by St. Columba. Ironically in the same year, these raiders from Scandanavia also plundered Iona, the most famous, scholarly, and elaborate of the monasteries founded by St. Columba. These Vikings then went back to their homeland carrying tales of wealth and land.

In 823, several groups returned. One party raided the monastery at Skellig Michel, off the coast of County Kerry, killing all the monks living there. Others raided the coasts of Wales, Cornwall, and Gaul, especially the area later to become known as Normandy (French for lands of the Norse). Their longboats were very fast and didn't draw much water, therefore they could sail right up onto the beaches, and also up the many rivers and streams.

Around 835 they sailed up the River Liffey and eventually came to the place where the Liffey meets a smaller stream, the River Poddle. There was a Celtic village located there and the Norsemen were impressed with its location and the fertility of the soil. The Vikings were not only interested in plunder and booty, they were also interested in trade, and the establishment of homes and trading centers. In 837, they constructed an earthen fort there on the highest hill (which is now the location of Dublin Castle and a portion of the Viking settlement is still located under the castle). They named the area Dubhlinn, meaning "Black Pool", after the dark color of the water found in the bog. The Norsemen minted silver coins here, the first ever produced in Ireland. For the next two hundred years Dublin would remain a city of Norsemen and Danes. Remember, the Irish Capital at that time was Armagh.

Originally sixty ships had sailed up the Liffey and another sixty had sailed up the River Boyne, all under the command of Tuirgeis (also called Thorgest in historical literature), who was one of the most famous and capable leaders in Nordic history. Tuirgeis next headed for the Irish capital of Armagh where he drove out the followers of St. Patrick around the year 845. He converted the church into a pagan temple and declared himself the High Priest. He next set off for Clonmacnoise, Ireland's second most holy city, and did the same thing there. He placed his wife Otta on the throne there and she supposedly declared herself High Priestess and daily screamed scathing oracles and magical incantations, insulting and condemning the Irish.

Shortly after this, still in 845, Tuirgeis was taken prisoner by Malachy (or Maelsechlainn in Irish), King of Meath, and drowned in Loch Owel, supposedly an act of the Irish Saints. The remaining Norsemen had to fight all the way up the River Shannon and across to the Sligo coast where their ships were waiting. Tuirgeis' followers were almost exclusively of Norwegian background.

Meanwhile the Danes, who were more organized than the Norse, were plundering England and had established their capital in Northumbria–at

York. In 847, the Danes invaded the east coast of Ireland with about fifty ships. At first the Irish called all these invaders "Genti", meaning Heathen, or "Lochlannaigh"(meaning "Men of the Lakes"- as does the word "Viking"). But they soon began distinguishing between the Lochlannaigh and the "Danair". The Norwegians, or Lochlannaigh, were also called the White Heathens, and the Danes, or Danair, were also called the "Black Heathens", primarily because of the color of their hair.

In 850, the Danes seized and plundered Dublin. In 852, the Norwegians regained control, under their mighty warlord known as "Amahlaobh" in Irish, or "Olaf the White" throughout most other historical accounts. The Norwegians then established several other settlements along the east coast, including Strangford and Carlingford in the north of Ireland, and Waterford, Wicklow, Cork, and Wexford in the south. Gradually, these coastal cities became more important and influential than the interior cities, such as Tara and Armagh. In the second half of the Ninth Century, the Danes sailed up the River Shannon and founded the city of Limerick, which flourished and came to exert great influence throughout that region.

Both of these peoples were slowly adopting Christianity as they avidly intermarried with the native Irish (many of the Norse took Christianity back to Scandanavia with them, and a grandson of "Olaf the White", Olaf II, became "Saint Olaf", the Patron Saint of Norway, canonized in 1164). The Norsemen assimilated the Irish ways more readily and quickly than the Danes, and eventually even became allies with the Irish against the Danes.

During the first part of the Tenth Century, the Danes came to control large portions of the interior of Ireland. In 914, Danish reinforcements arrived at Waterford and they sailed up the Shannon River again all the way to Lough Ree, plundering and burning everything not Danish, including Clonmacnoise. Their leader was Tomrair, the son of the King of Denmark. Most history texts claim that Tomrair died a horrible death, duly deserved.

King Cellachan of Cashel, whose reign as King of Munster began in 934, won back from the Danish invaders most of the Munster lands over the next decade. Cellachan was captured in 949, and rescued during the famous sea battle in the Bay of Dundalk in 950-951. The Danish Leader, Sitric, was drowned in this battle. Cellachan then proceeded directly to Dublin, overthrew the Danes there and, according to historical accounts took great quantities of Danish booty.

The most famous figure of the Danish Period, and one of the most famous in Irish History, was of course Brian Boru. He was born Brian mac Cenneidigh (son of Kennedy) in 941. He took the name of Boru from a town of which he was very fond located on the banks of the River Shannon. He was the youngest of twelve brothers. Ten of these brothers would be killed in battle. One of his brothers, Mahon, seized the throne of Cashel in 964. In 976, Brian at age thirty-five would become King of Munster and in three years would become the king of all of southern Ireland.

In 999, Brian united with Malachy II, his former rival, to defeat the Danes near Dunlavin in County Wicklow. Historical accounts claim that over seven thousand Danes were killed there. Brian and Malachy then plundered and again burned Dublin. Malachy and Brian then again quarreled and in 1002, after Malachy discovered defections in his military ranks and conceded, Brian became the High King of all of Ireland. The Ui Neill dynasty also yielded the high kingship to him without a fight.

After driving the Danes from Ulster and reclaiming Armagh in 1004, his Scribe, Maelsuthain, wrote in the Book of Armagh that Brian was "Emperor of the Irish". Brian was an exceptional warrior and strategist, he built roads and churches, built schools and encouraged learning, and even sent emissaries all over the world to buy books.

Brian made a pact with the Dublin Danes and in exchange for their loyalty they were given land. Brian gave his daughter in marriage to Sigtryggr, his former opponent and leader of the Dublin Danes, and Brian himself married Sigtryggr's mother, Gormlaith, who according to history was exceptionally beautiful and seduced many men, being married five or six times—rather in the Cleopatra tradition (Brian was either her second or third husband). After Brian eventually got rid of her, she developed a deep hatred and was the eventual cause of Brian's death.

In 1014, Brian was seventy-three years old and facing the final great battle against the remaining foreign adversaries, who had gathered on the east coast near Clontarf with reinforcements from Normandy, Flanders, England, Cornwall, the Orkneys, the Shetlands, and the Hebrides. Brian wanted to lead the fight, but was persuaded by his son and his generals to remain behind the lines in a tent, under heavy guard.

Both armies were estimated to be approximately 20,000 men, but the Danish troops were much better armed and equipped. The Danes were winning at first, but then Malachy showed up with reinforcements and the tide was turned in favor of the Irish. As the Dane's were fleeing, Brian's guards were overrun and Brian was killed. Brian's whereabouts supposedly had been disclosed by Gormlaith. Brian supposedly killed his assassin, Brodar, before he died.

The next year, 1015, Malachy defeated the last of the hostile foreigners near Dublin and reigned in peace as High King of Ireland, until his death in 1022. All the Danes and Vikings that remained in Ireland then became peaceful, settled down, intermarried, and history says they became "more Irish than the Irish". They severed their ties with Scandanavia, gave up their pagan beliefs, and came to be known in Ireland as "Ostman" (men of the east). This is something that would soon anger the Norsemen's relatives, the Normans, who had much more easily gained control of southern England and the coast of France.

The Irish gave the Norsemen Christianity, civility, culture and language. The Norsemen taught the Irish their advanced shipbuilding skills (In Irish, virtually every word regarding shipbuilding or the parts of ships was originally a Norse word). The great shipyards of Donegal (In Irish "Dun na nGall", or "Fort of Foreigners") were established by these Norsemen; and, if there is yet today any predominantly Viking-influenced area in Ireland, it would be Donegal. The language dialect there is distinctly different and heavily Norse influenced.

All was rather peaceful for the next hundred-and-fifty years or so, until Henry II, the Norman King of England decided the Irish may revert back to their pagan ways and asked the English Pope, Nicholas Breakspeare, whom was now known as Adrian IV, permission to invade the island for the purpose of saving these poor wretched Irish souls.

Adrian IV, who was born in 1100 and reigned as Pope from 1154-1159, was the only Englishman to ever become Pope and he quickly issued the Papal Bull "Laudabiliter" authorizing Henry II to conquer the island of Ireland for the purpose of relieving the deplorable religious conditions and lack of morals.

The Norman English:

The Normans were basically Vikings or Norsemen who had conquered the coastal region of Gaul, or modern-day France, and had been living there for a couple hundred years. They so dominated the region that in 911, King Charles III of France ceded the land to them, and the Norse king, Rollo, became the first Duke of Normandy. In exchange they agreed to give up piracy, adopt Christianity, as well as the customs and language of the French. Norman is the French equivalent of Norseman, and the region came to be called Normandie (lands of the Norse).

In 1066, the Anglo-Saxon king of England, Edward (The Confessor), died without an heir. His mother was a Norman. Edward's final words indicated that he wanted William, the Duke of Normandy, to succeed him. William was the illegitimate son of the former Duke of Normandy, Robert I, and a peasant girl. He was known throughout most of history as "William the Bastard" (but I suppose this became politically incorrect so it was changed to "William the Conqueror"). The Anglo-Saxon assembly of England ignored King Edward's decree and named Harold Godwinsson the new king. This brought an immediate reaction from the very powerful

Normans, and on 14 October, 1066, the forces of William defeated those of Godwinsson at the Battle of Hastings, and England became Norman with William being crowned King of England at Westminster Abbey on Christmas Day, 1066. Henry II was the great-grandson of William (and the first of the Plantagenet dynasty which would rule England until the death of Richard III in 1485).

Henry II was actually asked by one of the Irish kings, Diarmuid MacMurrough, to invade Ireland and restore him as King of Leinster. He had been ousted because he had abducted another king's wife, by the name of Dervorgilla, in 1152. Several historical accounts stated she went along quite willingly, but whatever the case, much of history also says he stole her. Henry was at the time fighting in French Aquitaine and couldn't be bothered, but gave Diarmuid a letter stating that any of the Norman warlords were welcome to help Diarmuid (Dermot) if they so desired.

Richard de Clare was the Norman/Welsh "Earl of Pembroke" and he was going broke. He was also known as "Strongbow", and he agreed to help MacMurrough in exchange for land, and MacMurrough's beautiful daughter's hand in marriage. Strongbow first sent to Ireland his two half-brothers, Robert Fitz Stephen and Maurice Fitz Gerald in the spring of 1169, with about four hundred archers and knights (Strongbow followed within the year). They were joined by MacMurrough's army of about five hundred and captured the Danish city of Wexford (on the third try).

Foreign mercenaries had always been brought into Ireland; and, as long as it didn't directly affect the other kings, these kings really didn't pay much attention.

Diarmuid then attacked another Danish city, Dublin. This got a little more attention, and King Roderick O'Connor then gathered an army. O'Connor was joined by about four hundred Waterford men, and they attacked the Norman forces. They were badly routed due to the Normans' superior weaponry and armor. The Normans took over forty prisoners, broke their arms and legs, and hurled them over the cliffs and into the sea.

This got even more attention and a short time later Strongbow showed up with about twelve hundred more men.

The Normans then attacked Waterford, slaughtering most of the inhabitants. Strongbow married Diarmuid's daughter on the battlefield, standing in blood to glorify his victory, according to historic accounts. He then declared himself the King of Leinster, somewhat settled down and became quite comfortable. He liked Ireland and would not return to Normandy when summoned by King Henry II.

We mentioned earlier about Henry being upset by the fact that the previous Norsemen had settled out in Ireland becoming quite content, and according to history became "more Irish than the Irish". He was worried that the same thing might possibly be happening to Strongbow and his followers. This, along with the fact he had heard about Ireland's great beauty and fertility, made Henry decide to visit there himself. He took four hundred ships and nearly five thousand knights and soldiers, and landed at Waterford in October of 1171. Most of the Irish chiefs were then forced to submit to Henry's authority, as they could provide no match for the Normans' superior military machine.

Henry then marched to Dublin and there set up his court, built a palace, and partied all winter long. He was a strong and brutal enforcer. In March 1172, he called a synod at Cashel where the Irish Bishops were forced to acknowledge Henry as "Lord Supreme" in Ireland. At Easter, Henry returned to England, leaving Strongbow in charge of Leinster, and others in charge elsewhere.

The Irish soon realized they had to do something, and began a campaign of subversion and gorilla warfare-type tactics. The Normans were brutal, burning the monasteries, killing entire villages, and building castles to protect themselves. Most of the castles still seen in Ireland yet today, were built during this period.

In 1185, King Henry II appointed nineteen-year-old Prince John as "Lord of Ireland". He was young, abrasive, insulting, and obnoxious. He was permitted to stay for only a short period; and, in that time he seriously damaged the English cause and greatly strengthened and united the Irish cause.

The English royal house has quite often been rather turbulent over the years, to put it mildly. Henry II died in 1189, cursing his entire family. He had held his wife, Eleanor of Aquitaine, a prisoner for over ten years because he believed that she had plotted with three of his five sons to over-throw him; and, he hated his sons, two of whom would become future Kings of England, Richard ("The Lionheart"), who upon the death of Henry became King of England in 1189, and John, who became king in 1199 while Richard was away on The Third Crusade and languishing in a Germanic prison after being taken captive by the Holy Roman Emperor, Henry VI. John took the throne in 1199, the same year that Donal MacCarthy of Desmond defeated the English of Munster and drove them from Limerick and the surrounding areas.

King John's Viceroy of Ireland, and Archbishop of Dublin, was a fellow named Henry of London. His only two passions were hunting deer and collecting money. He fleeced money from the English and the Irish alike. In order to build Dublin Castle, he closed several churches and confis-cated their property, including the great center of learning, Glendalough, which was revered throughout Europe for its sanctity, scholarship, and as a major center for the study of both Greek and Latin. Henry of London became nicknamed "The Scorch Villain".

The Irish would still be deterred from neither their religious beliefs nor their culture, and more and more of the Normans were realizing the Irish ways were more peaceful and truthful than those of the Normans. They noted that while the Brehon Laws were used in Ireland, there was never one instance of a Brehon (judge) being corrupt, or taking a bribe, or favor-ing his friends and family. All decisions were based on honor, truth, and honesty, and all the Irish happily accepted whatever ruling came down from the Brehons. This amazed the Normans, whose courts were based almost exclusively on favoritism and bribery. More and more Normans intermarried with the Irish, adopted Irish dress, language and customs; and, fostered their children to Irish families and Scholars.

This worried and infuriated the proud and arrogant Normans and led to the institution of the Penal Laws, among the first and most famous of which were the "Statutes of Kilkenny" passed in 1366-1367. These forbade Norman-Irish intermarriages, the wearing of Irish clothing, the speaking of the Irish language, the display of any Irish customs such as music and dance, and even included a law passed by Parliament that forbade moustaches. The Irish and the rest of Europe found moustaches fashionable at this time, but the Normans all had clean-shaven upper lips and tried to demand the Irish do the same. The formal penalties for violation of the Penal Laws included death, quartering and disembowelment. These Normans, however, never realized the strength and determination of the Irish, as virtually none of the invaders of Ireland have up until this very day, and the Irish never attempted to comply with these laws. This harsh treatment only furthered the Irish cause, determination, resolve, and resilience.

Medieval Ireland

With all the attempted restrictions and the oppression intended by the Penal Laws, the actual lifestyles and activities of the Irish kings and warlords was disrupted and changed very little in the beginning. The Irish chieftain was in reality still a semi-nomadic person. They spent a great deal of time out-of-doors, herding cattle and moving to better pastures, hunting, or engaging in feasts and celebrations. The native Irish were very close to nature and felt more comfortable out in the open. The Irish chieftains habitually dined out-of-doors, in the tradition of the ancient Celtic warriors (or fianna), and continued to do so well into Elizabethan times, much to the horror of the more "refined" English populace. The English also thought that the diet of the Irish was barbaric and scandalous as they ate under-cooked meat, raw salads and greens, milk, cheese, and other dairy products, while eating very little bread. In the face of Norman advances, if an Irish noble or chieftain were forced to flee to the woods, their material situation would in fact change very little. This allowed for great resilience, an important quality that would serve the Irish well throughout their history. All noble Irish families also maintained the services of a poet, whose task it was to record and preserve the legends and folktales, as well as keeping the positive aspects of recovery forever present in the hearts and minds of the people.

As was previously mentioned, the Royal Family of England was at this time having an abundance of problems on virtually every front. Their problems certainly didn't die with Henry II. When his son John became king in 1199, the monarchy was faced with revolt from the people due to the extremely heavy tax burden the people had been forced to bear in order to support the ridiculous Crusades; and, even worse to ransom

Richard from his captor, the Holy Roman Emperor Henry VI. In 1209, the Pope, Innocent III, excommunicated King John, and forced him to make several humiliating concessions to regain favor, including reducing England to the status of a Vatican fiefdom. The people of England didn't care for this at all, but the final straw was when the French defeated the English at the Battle of Bouvines in 1214. John was overthrown and forced to sign the Magna Carta in 1215, which dramatically reduced the powers of the monarchy. Most of the people wanted to completely dissolve the monarchy at this time, but it survived by a thread, with this being an extremely important point regarding future events in Ireland and elsewhere.

A rebellious and dissident Irish population also posed a direct threat to the English crown, and in 1263, the crown of Ireland was offered to Haakon IV of Norway, a strong English ally, but he died before being able to accept.

A counter to the great Norman fighting machine had been forming in the highlands of northern Scotland. They were families of professional soldiers, of a Norse/Gaelic derivative, known as "galloglasses" ("galloglaigh" in Irish, meaning "foreign troops"). They were highly trained and specialized, heavily armed, and the Irish chieftains began importing them for protection.

Needless to say the English were not free to vigorously enforce the Irish Penal Laws with much enthusiasm. The Irish for the most part ignored them, meeting at times with just enough brutality to reinforce the Irish resolve. For example, there were laws passed forbidding the Irish from engaging in trade, commerce, or becoming a member of any of the guilds, but by the Fifteenth Century the native Irish made up the majority in the Craft and Merchant Guilds. However, the bulk of the very important international markets and commerce were still controlled by the English. There were pockets of Irish Merchants in Italy, Spain, and especially France, but these accounted for a rather small percentage overall.

In 1348 and 1349, the Black Death decimated Ireland, as it did much of England and the continent, and by the beginning of the Fifteenth Century, the English sphere of authority and influence was limited to a small strip of land approximately thirty miles long and twenty miles deep along the coast surrounding Dublin, known as "The Pale", and a few walled cities in the north.

The tales of the voyages of St. Brendan were especially popular during this period, and inspired Christopher Columbus and others to set sail looking for new and wonderful lands. North America, Central America, and the West Indies were even called "Great Ireland" during this period in much of the literature. I believe it was previously mentioned that Christopher Columbus even visited Ireland and studied closely the notes of St. Brendan before beginning his voyage. He also took a number of Irishmen along with him (Patrick Maguire was the Irishman accompanying Christopher Columbus, who was supposedly the first to set foot on the new world).

Through this period the Irish also maintained their thirst for scholarship. The University of Paris was the major worldwide university at this time, closely followed by the University of Bologna, and both of these had a large concentration of Irish students, especially the University of Paris. Irish students were among the best of Europe regarding matters of Astronomy, Geography, and Medicine. Remember, every Irish Gaelic Chieftain, and nearly every Irish Lord employed an astronomer, geographer, and physician, as well as a poet or bard. It is interesting to note that Duke Lionel, brother of the King of England, and sponsor of the Kilkenny Statutes, which had basically banned or forbidden virtually everything "Irish", employed only Irish physicians and would let no other touch him. All during the Middle Ages, Ireland was known as the land of Saints and Scholars, and to this day is still referred to as such in much of the current academic literature.

Still at this time, the Norman-English were intermarrying with the Irish and ever more adopting many of the Irish ways. The Norman family of the Geraldines, who became the extremely Irish "Fitzgeralds", played a major role in the history of Ireland. The Geraldines of Kildare held lands all the way from County Down in the north, to at least County Carlow in the south, and west to Limerick. They ruled the area of Desmond in south Munster as an independent Monarchy. They even maintained their own Navy.

The Geraldines were also Great Scholars and intermingled with the Irish Scholars enthusiastically, again intermarrying and adopting the Irish lifestyle as we've mentioned. They promoted all academic endeavors and even tried to establish another National University in the tradition of the University of Armagh, following its destruction (It had been the greatest center of European learning until the beginning of the Thirteenth Century, employing as many as 5,000 scholars from everywhere in the known world). Gerald, the Earl of Kildare's, new university was called "The College of the Blessed Virgin Mary at Maynooth". This Geraldine assimilation of the Irish ways again brought avid displeasure to the English.

Gerald, the Eighth Earl of Kildare, who reigned from 1477 until 1513, was called "Gerald the Great" by the Irish. He was viewed at the time, as well as through most of history, as the unofficial king of Ireland during this period. The Ninth Earl of Kildare, Gerait Og (also known as "Gerald the Younger"), was educated in England, appointed "Lord Deputy" of Ireland by his cousin Henry VIII in 1513, but in the end would become even more passionately Irish than his father had been. He was removed by Henry after seven years and charged by the English with sedition and conspiracy.

From history we learn that Henry VIII had a very rough time from his earliest days. His father, Henry VII, was a rather demanding old fellow who had betrothed Henry to Catherine of Aragon, the daughter of King Ferdinand and Queen Isabella of Spain, only a few days before Henry VIII received the crown as King of England. Catherine had been the wife of Henry VIII's brother, Arthur, who had met an untimely death. Henry's father wanted to keep the political alliance in tact between Spain and England, hence Henry's marriage to Catherine was arranged. Catherine had several miscarriages and stillbirths and by 1527, their union had not produced any male heirs; and, only one female, Mary. Henry knew that the marriage of a man to his brother's wife was prohibited by biblical, canon and secular law (his marriage had required a special dispensation from Pope Julius II); and, he was convinced that God had cursed this union with Catherine. By 1527, he had decided to rid himself of Catherine and marry one of her ladies in waiting, Anne Boleyn. He wanted the Pope to grant an annulment but this was virtually impossible because Pope Clement VII was at that time being held prisoner by Charles V of the Holy Roman Empire; and, Charles V just happened to be Catherine's nephew. Henry was very confused, stressed out, and frustrated and he took out much of this frustration eventually on the Irish and all other Catholics. He renounced Catholicism and formed the Anglican Church of England.

Anyway, Gerait Og, the Earl of Kildare, was reappointed by Henry to the position of Lord Deputy of Ireland in 1525, to the people's delight; but, it was soon discovered that he had formed a secret alliance with Francis I, King of France, in 1523, to overthrow the English and drive them from Ireland and Scotland. The insurrection was delayed however when the Scottish troops under the Duke of Albany failed to show up and the Earl of Kildare was summoned back to England, charged with being a traitor, and held in the Tower of London for the next six years. In 1532, Gerait was again reinstated in Ireland, as many around Henry convinced him that it was to his political advantage to do so. However, in 1534, more charges were brought against him and he returned to the Tower of London for the last time. He died there.

His son, Lord Thomas (also known as "Silken Thomas"–for the silk scarves he and his followers wore), rebelled in Ireland, riding through the streets of Dublin with about 150 men declaring Irish Independence. At first he won a few battles, but then the English sent more troops, he was captured, hanged, drawn, and quartered, along with supposedly all the male members of his family. The English believed the Geraldine bloodline had been exterminated, and through the Act of Parliament in 1537, decreed all Geraldine lands were now forfeited to the Crown.

However, two children survived, and in one of them, Gerald Fitzgerald, then age twelve, Ireland would come to place her future hope. His aunt, Lady Eleanor Fitzgerald, secretly nursed and raised the boy, and then with great courage and conviction, united all the families of Ireland, both Gael and Shan Gall (the new foreign settlers), into a vast confederacy against the English. All past tribal conflicts and political disagreements were put aside and Ireland hoped by the beginning of the Seventeenth Century to virtually live as one nation, united in a common language, literature, religion, custom, music, and suffering. Gerald was conveyed to France to assure his security, and when Henry VIII learned of this, he sent his best friend, Lord Leonard Gray, Deputy of Ireland, to the gallows for allowing the boy to escape.

The hope of Ireland rested in Gerald, and everywhere he went in France, Italy, and the Lowland Countries he was praised, followed by cheering crowds, and proclaimed the "King of Ireland". He was given the finest education known, studying with the Bishop of Verona among others. He was courted by all of Europe's leaders, including the Holy Roman Emperor, Charles V, and the new Pope, Paul III. It seemed not too many people cared for the English and King Henry VIII.

The French, Scots, and Irish were preparing for an invasion to liberate Ireland when the English, recognizing this, proposed the marriage of Mary Queen of Scots to their king-to-be, Edward VI, (which was basically accomplished by force) and at the last minute this symbolically united these two countries, Scotland and England. The French and Irish were originally hoping that Gerald was going to wed Mary. About this same time, the French King Francis I died, and Henry II became King of France. He had wanted Mary to wed his son. Consequently, all invasion plans were abandoned.

Gerald then submitted to Mary and petitioned her to reinstate his lands and title, which she did in part. These would then again be the center of various Irish revolts and rebellions, with Gerald as the leader and hero. Unfortunately, by this time the English had employed heavy artillery, the "Great Gray Guns", and the Irish could not match this weaponry.

King Edward VI, son of Henry VIII and Jane Seymour, Henry's third wife (Anne Boleyn was executed in 1536 for alleged treason and adultery), died in 1553, and was succeeded by Mary I, daughter of Henry VIII and his first wife Catherine, who was an avid Catholic. Edward had tried to place Lady Jane Grey, a protestant, on the throne but she only lasted a few days, was overthrown and beheaded. Mary I tried to restore Catholicism with the same brutal violence that her father had used to promote Protestantism. She executed at least three hundred of the Protestant leaders (burning them at the stake) and sent hundreds more scurrying into exile in Germany, Switzerland, and in the case of John Knox, into Scotland. From there they plotted the restoration of Protestant England, and inspired a hatred of Catholicism that remains in many to this very day.

Mary's reign offered a welcomed reprieve and respite for Ireland, but it did not last long. When Mary married the Catholic Spanish Prince Philip (later to become King Philip II of Spain), her days were numbered. Following Mary's death in 1558, her half-sister, Elizabeth I, daughter of Henry VIII and Anne Boleyn, became Queen of England. Elizabeth I had previously been declared illegitimate by her father Henry, but nonetheless she resumed her father's policies (she apparently was never bothered also by the fact that he had beheaded her mother). Her violent treatment and attempted extermination of the Irish are well documented, as is evidenced by the fact that she demanded the heads of Irish Rebels, such as that of Shane O'Neill, as well as the heads of Irish Priests, be brought to her for examination, and then impaled and placed on display in London and else-where.

There were countless acts of brutality and slaughter documented during the reigns of Henry VIII, Edward VI, and Elizabeth I, as well as horrific laws enacted by the English Parliament that called for the extermination of the Irish, who were quite often not even considered humans. And consequently, there was always the underlying current of Irish rebellion and desire for independence, personified in the great Irish heroes, such as Shane O'Neill, Hugh O'Neill, Hugh O'Donnell (also known as "Red Hugh"), and Rory O'Moore among others.

Shane O'Neill was descended from the High Kings of Ireland and was the chieftain of Tyrone in northwest Ulster. He was also known as "Shane the Proud". When his father, Conn the Lame, accepted the English title of Baron of Dungannon, Shane went into rebellion. Upon his father's deathbed he killed his half-brother whom would have become the new Baron, and reclaimed the lands for the Irish. He was an excellent soldier and won several battles over the English. Queen Elizabeth tried everything to subdue him. She even attempted to act as if she would honor, acknowledge his claims, and make friends with him. She then attempted to poison him and his entire family, but the poisoner was unskilled and they all lived. Shane then knew with whom he dealt and became ever more determined. Queen Elizabeth sent three hundred English soldiers and several hundred mercenaries against Shane, who proceeded to kill them all. The English soldiers had worn these new scarlet coats into battle, and this battle was ever after called the "Battle of the Red Coats". In 1567, Shane was invited to a banquet given by Sorley Boy McDonnell, another Ulster nobleman whom Shane had once defeated. Queen Elizabeth and her Lord Deputy, Sussex, planted an assassin at the banquet and when all the men became drunk, he killed Shane and cut off his head. His head was then taken to Queen Elizabeth and later impaled and displayed upon the northwest gate of Dublin.

Hugh O'Neill and Hugh O'Donnell (Red Hugh) formed an alliance in the last years of the Sixteenth Century that led to the "Nine Years' War"(1592-1601) and the near complete expulsion of the English from

Ulster. Hugh O'Donnell had been the heir to the lands of the Tir-Conaill and was captured by the English at the age of fourteen and held in the Tower of Birmingham at Dublin Castle along with the two sons of Shane O'Neill, Henry and Art. They made a daring escape in the dead of winter, but Art and Henry both died from exposure. It was then that Red Hugh united with Hugh O'Neill and fought the Nine Years' War, which eventually drove the English from Ulster. A Treaty was proposed that restored to the Irish their lands, but Queen Elizabeth died an insane maniac before the treaty could be signed. While on a trip to Spain, Red Hugh was poisoned by an agent of the English Lord Deputy. Hugh O'Neill was betrayed and falsely accused by the English as they placed a bounty on his life. He was forced to flee from Ireland in 1607 along with approximately fifty other noblemen and Irish Chieftains in what has come to be known as the "Flight of the Earls".

Rory O'Moore was the chief man responsible for the "Rising of 1641" in Ulster that led to the rumors of the "Popish Massacre". This will all be discussed further in the next lecture.

The Sixteenth Century was also the period of the Reformation and the English monarchy made every effort to force the Irish to accept their new protestant religion, including the closing of all Catholic churches and the confiscation of their properties; and, the mandated murdering of Priests. But the Irish, with their deeply spiritual and academic religious history, were never going to recognize the murderous and treacherous Henry or Elizabeth as the head of the church.

The Seventeenth Century

The Seventeenth Century began with the full-blown rebellion mentioned in the last lecture, the "Nine Years' War", at first showing favorably for the Irish. It was a war of both independence and religion, and the Irish looked to the then greatest Catholic nation on earth for assistance, Spain. The aforementioned Hugh O'Neill in Ulster and Red Hugh O'Donnell in Connacht, were winning regularly against the English, basically through the use of superior tactics and strategies, and expelling the English from area after area.

In 1599, O'Neill took control of Armagh, and with it, Ulster. For allowing this to happen, Queen Elizabeth, beheaded one of her favorite and most capable generals, and reported courtier, Lord Essex. Most of the remaining English troops were now located in Munster, exactly where the Spanish reinforcements made landfall, at Kinsale. O'Neill had told the Spanish to make landfall in Ulster with at least five thousand men. They only brought three thousand and were under the command of a general, named d'Aquila, with somewhat questionable capabilities. They were immediately surrounded by the English and lost a battle they should have easily won—a battle that would have most likely assured Irish Independence.

O'Neill had fought his way south in an attempt to reach the Spanish, now he had to fight his way back to Ulster, fighting all the way in unfamiliar territory. His army had been in reality quite devastated, yet the English weren't aware of this and proposed a treaty, restoring his and other Irish lands in 1602. Before the treaty could be signed however, Queen Elizabeth died on 23 March 1603, a raving madwoman by most accounts.

King James VI of Scotland, son of Mary Stuart, Queen of Scots, then became King James I of England, and refused to both sign the treaty and restore Irish lands. He then circulated a forged document, purportedly written by O'Neill, which claimed O'Neill and his followers were planning another rebellion that would eventually overthrow the entire English monarchy. Every English Lord promised an army and O'Neill knew that their struggle was for now lost and his only safety, and that of his followers, was in fleeing to the continent, where they would be welcomed in Spain, Rome, Brussels, and elsewhere. He also knew there were numerous Irish soldiers in the service of these countries, and perhaps he could raise an army that would return to Ireland and secure independence.

In Irish history this is known as the "Flight of the Earls", and ushers in another very dark period. The leaders of many of the Irish royal families left in 1607, most settling in Rome where they were treated like royalty by Pope Paul V. When Hugh O'Neill died in 1616, he was given a royal funeral and buried in the Church of San Pietro on the Janiculum Hill, a site reserved for only the most prestigious of royalty.

Within a decade following the Flight of the Earls, King James devised a plan that has influenced Irish life to this very day. It was the development of the "Ulster Plantation". James decreed that all lands belonging to the Earls that had left now belonged to the English crown. In reality these lands never had belonged to the individuals, but belonged to the entire clan community, but they were now deeded over to England. Over four-million acres were confiscated, then re-deeded to English settlers in one-thousand and two-thousand acre plots, and the true Irish owners were either driven off or murdered. The Irish were forced to live like animals in the woods, feeding on leaves, roots, and berries. Many fled to the continent and even America. There was a substantial migration of Irish into North Carolina, Georgia, and somewhat Virginia (Virginia was a bit more English—remember it was given by Queen Elizabeth to one of her courtiers, Sir Walter Raleigh, who then named it for his "virgin" queen). (Note: We're currently building a beautiful mountaintop special interest school in the mountains of western North Carolina, and this entire region was originally settled by the Irish and Scots-Irish over three-hundred-and-fifty years ago).

As I'm certain you're all well aware by now, the Irish were not about to starve to death and die in the bogs. Their wrath and displeasure with the British were growing daily. The "Rising of 1641" was the natural outcome of these injustices. It was a result mostly of the efforts of Rory O'Moore, from County Offaly, whom for years secretly and patiently worked to unite the Irish families and the exiled Irish soldiers and officers in an effort to overthrow the British and drive them from Ireland forever. The Rising was planned to overwhelm the British of Ulster on the night of 21 October 1641, and that is exactly what it did. The British landholders were forced to flee into the few walled cities they could hold, basically Derry, Belfast, and Enniskillen, and in one night the Irish pretty much reclaimed the entire province.

Unfortunately, only Ulster rose up that night. There originally were plans for the other regions to do the same. The armies led by O'Moore, Macguire and MacMahon were supposed to overtake Dublin Castle, but these plans were revealed to the English by a traitor; and, Macguire and MacMahon were killed and Rory O'Moore barely escaped.

Current research indicates very few English were killed during the Rising, probably mostly only those who had brought it on through their particular actions. Most families were simply told to leave. But in the years following, great stories developed outlining the atrocities of the great "Popish Massacre". The death toll kept mounting. The poet Milton, Cromwell's Secretary at the time, eventually wrote that 610,000 English had been brutally slaughtered by the "Catholics" (there were only approximately 200,000 English residing in the all of Ulster). Ten years after the Rising, the Cromwell Commission conducted hearings, and protestant ministers one after another testified to the slaughter they had witnessed. Most of these, it was later discovered, had not even been present. The "Irish Massacre of 1641" has even been perpetuated in numerous historical texts, when in fact it has been shown to be in reality pure fiction. At the time, however, it was politically advantageous for the Puritans to promote tales of such horrendous atrocities. This became fuel for Cromwell and his New Model Army who would soon kill and butcher in the name of the Lord.

Two factions of the English parliament had also been at odds for some time. In 1641, parliament issued Charles I with a list of over two hundred grievances against the crown, known as the "Grand Remonstrance". Charles then dissolved the parliament after invading it with soldiers on horseback. In 1642, the English parliamentary forces split and the English Civil War ensued, between Charles' "Cavaliers" and the Puritan "Roundheads". In 1646, the Roundheads won and in 1649 executed Charles I, at the fervent insistence of Cromwell (there's no doubt he liked killing). He then declared himself "Lord Protector" of England. He also bestowed upon himself the titles of "Commander-In-Chief", and "Lord Lieutenant of Ireland"; and, in 1649, he left for Ireland with his extremely modern and efficient "New Model Army" to avenge the atrocities of the "Popish Massacre".

The Irish had no defense for this ultra-modern, super-efficient, state-of-the-art killing machine. Cromwell and his men would be remembered in Ireland for all time! This army went first to Drogheda where they killed over three thousand soldiers and another thousand-plus townspeople, including women, children, and the elderly, who had sought shelter in and around the church. Cromwell's army basically wiped out the entire town of Drogheda. They went next to Wexford where they did the same thing, killing over two thousand. After Drogheda, Cromwell wrote to the parliament, "It has pleased God to bless our endeavor at Drogheda…I wish that all honest hearts may give the glory of this to God alone, to whom indeed the praise of this mercy belongs." Parliament declared 2 October 1649, as a day of Thanksgiving in honor of the great victory.

Cromwell failed on his first attempt to capture Waterford, and not wanting to waste the time, he moved on to Cork city, a much easier prey, mainly because, according to accounts, a large number of English protestants lived there and they handed the remainder of the city over to Cromwell. The best fight against Cromwell was displayed at Clonmel, where Hugh O'Neill, son of the aforementioned Hugh O'Neill, with only 1500 men, allowed Cromwell to enter the town, where the O'Neill forces surrounded them and killed over five-hundred of Cromwell's soldiers. Cromwell never could then capture the city after several attempts, and had to resort to a blockade, during which O'Neill's men a few at a time slipped away at night until they were all out of the city.

As well as these major cities, Cromwell's army destroyed scores of smaller towns and villages along their routes. Another aspect of their strategy or tactics was to destroy all the crops along the way hoping to starve those who remained. The army had with them large numbers of scythes and cut down, then burned, all the crops. In eight months, Cromwell had devastated a good portion of the island. In May 1650, he returned to England.

He left an army in Ireland, under the command of at first general Ireton and then upon his death, Cromwell's son Henry took over. The cities that had not been conquered, such as Kilkenny, Waterford, Galway, and Limerick, had negotiated "settlements", and on 12 May 1652, the controversial "Articles of Kilkenny"(basically signed by two pro-English factions) were signed putting an end to probably the worst period in all of Ireland's rather tragic history.

Although most of the killing was ended, the suffering of the Irish People was far from over. Through what is known as the "Cromwellian Settlement", all Irish lands east of the River Shannon were forfeited to the English, and the Irish were ordered to "Hell or Connacht" (by act of parliament and under penalty of death, no Irish person was to be found east of the Shannon River after 1 May, 1654). The land in Connacht is the worst in all of Ireland, containing more rocks than soil. Cromwell himself made the comment that in Connacht there was, "not enough wood to hang a man, not enough water to drown a man, and not enough soil to cover his corpse". This again stimulated a major migration—to the armies, trades, and universities of continental Europe, and again also to America.

As if this all wasn't enough, the plague hit Ireland in 1652 and 1653, probably due, at least in part, to the carnage and decay. Following this period various historians have estimated that between two-thirds and five-sixths of the Irish population had been either exterminated, or had left the country. Even after all this, the Irish People survived, revived, and came back even stronger. Cromwell died in 1658.

In 1660, Charles II, son of Charles I, was asked to return to the throne amid great rejoicing. Most of the English were tired of the staunch, "holier-than-thou", and extremely judgmental attitudes of the Puritans. Many of these however were still present in the parliament and battled with Charles often, even devising the "Popish Plot"(which was basically a false rumor that the Queen and Irish Catholics were going to kill Charles, so his brother James, the Duke of York and a catholic, could take over the throne). They even tried to pass legislation that would forbid James from ever taking the throne. Well, the pro-Charles forces won out, many of the Puritans were arrested or exiled, and in 1685, upon the death of Charles II, James took the throne as King James II, but as we shall see, the battles were not yet over.

James II versus William of Orange:

When James II took the throne of England in 1685, one of his very first acts was to suspend the Penal Laws. He was a catholic and this act struck terror in the hearts of the Puritans and protestant England. They well remembered the earlier actions of Mary I, as she sought vengeance for the atrocities that had been perpetuated against Catholics. They also of course believed in the horrors of the "Popish Massacre".

James appointed Richard Talbot, also known as the "Duke of Tyrconnell" to oversee affairs in Ireland. He was a large powerful man who had been at Drogheda, a lad of sixteen, when Cromwell came through. He immediately removed all Puritans from the ranks of the military and replaced them, both officers and soldiers, with Irish Catholics. Three thousand of these Irish Catholic soldiers were sent to England to reinforce James' army there. Their arrival in England was met with panic.

English protestant agents began communicating with one William, head of the House of Orange, in the Netherlands, who had a bloodline connection to the English throne. Louis XIV in France sent messengers to James advising him that he should beware of this connection. James actually resented these accusations because, after all, William was married to James' daughter, Mary.

In 1688, James' wife gave birth to a son, thus assuring a Catholic heir to the throne. This was more than the English Protestants could bare, and they invited William of Orange to invade England and overthrow the monarchy of James II. In November 1688, William arrived in England and met virtually no opposition. James' army melted away, his friends and family deserted him, and William was welcomed with a great celebration by the English people. This is known as the "Glorious Revolution". James was forced to flee to the protection of Louis XIV in France.

William and Mary immediately acknowledged a "Bill of Rights" that limited the powers of the monarchy, assured the privileged status of the English elite, and prohibited any Roman Catholics from ever again ascending to the throne of England. (In 1701, the "Act of Settlement" stated that if no heirs survived Anne, the second daughter of James and the last of the Stuart monarchs, that the throne of England would be passed to the protestant German House of Hanover—and that is exactly what happened. When Queen Anne died in 1714, having outlived all of her children, the "Elector" of the House of Hanover became King George I of England—he was the third foreign monarch to ascend to the English throne in just over a century, none of which could even speak English. George I never even visited England, considering it a wretched country.)

Catholics and the Irish soldiers who had been sent to England scrambled back to Ireland and prepared for a fight. Another false rumor was being circulated in England claiming that the Irish were slaughtering Protestants in Ireland. It was becoming obvious that the dispute for the English crown between James and William was going to be settled on Irish soil. Within two months over fifty thousand Irishmen enlisted in the Irish army, led by Tyrconnell. They were known by those in William's army as the "Irish Black Guard", a raggedy group with no uniforms, many not even wearing shoes.

Tyrconnell sent to France for James, declaring he must fight for the throne and this could best be accomplished from Ireland. James landed at Kinsale on the nineteenth of March 1689, with gold, arms, ammunition, and over four hundred French officers and sharpshooters. Tyrconnell met him at Cork and the combined armies marched northward, encountering basically no opposition on the march to Ulster, until they reached the town of Derry, where the city's apprentice boys slammed the city gates closed on James, screaming "no surrender". The siege of Derry lasted 109 days, during which time James became disgusted and went to Dublin. In Dublin, James was met with great enthusiasm, an Irish parliament was established, and plans were finalized for a more aggressive assault on Ulster.

William's army, however, arrived at Belfast in late summer, under the command of the Dutch general, Schomberg, and proceeded to attack Carrickfergus, finally capturing it following a week's siege. They sailed up the River Foyle and broke the siege/blockade at Derry. They then established their camp at Dundalk. The autumn rains were coming, disease was ravaging William's army, and the French generals were advising James to attack at that time, however he did not agree and forbade the attack. He even accused the French generals of trying to usurp his command and James angrily returned to Dublin. In March 1690, William then sent seven thousand more troops to reinforce Schomberg. They also brought the first recently invented machine guns, capable of firing the equivalent of 150 musket rounds per minute. In June, William came to join his troops, aware of the great importance of this struggle.

Meanwhile, James and his army abandoned their positions in the north which basically had William's armies surrounded, and retreated down the Boyne River. (It is said that James already had ships awaiting him at Waterford for the purpose of carrying him back to France, where he enjoyed the lavish lifestyle). The two armies met on 1 July 1690, with James' army inferior in both numbers (26,000 to over 36,000), and in weaponry.

The "Battle of the Boyne" raged all day with William's army slowly gaining ground. At five o'clock James fled for Dublin, arriving there at ten o'clock that night. At nightfall, the Irish army dissipated having no command, with the battle being fought virtually to a standstill. In Dublin, James stated that the Irish army had fled the battlefield and that he would never again lead an Irish army. He promptly then left for Waterford and sailed to France, never to again set foot on Irish soil.

The Irish however were determined to continue fighting, as their goal was far more important than the restoration of the Stuart monarchy. Their goal was Irish independence. The French generals wanted to seek favorable terms from William and then return to France. The bulk of the Irish army went to Limerick. The French general, Lauzun, went to Galway with the French soldiers and most of the guns and ammunition. William knew of the dissention and the French army's desire to return to France. He offered favorable terms to end the conflict.

The Irish had suffered far too greatly over the years behind the English promises of favorable terms. They were determined to never give in, prepared to die rather than yield. The Irish held out bravely through three sieges orchestrated by William's far more capable legions, and had even driven the English armies back into the bog. Meanwhile the cities of Cork and Kinsale had fallen to the English.

There was only one hope left for the English in Limerick, and that was to attempt to break through at the narrow Aughrim Pass, and it was well defended by the Irish's superior position from the Aughrim Castle. As the English advanced, it was discovered that the cases of bullets and cannon balls left for the Irish were not compatible with their muskets and canons. They tore up everything they had made of metal in an effort to provide ammunition, even the buttons off their coats, but were in the end no match for the English's superior weaponry.

The English again offered terms, but Limerick refused to quit and William's army again attacked on 23 September 1690. When they could not overtake the city, they turned the siege into a blockade, and again offered "favorable terms" as they were anxious to return to England, promising the Irish many freedoms, including that of religion and the restoration of their lands. The Irish leader, Sarsfield, did not trust the English and demanded that the treaty be signed by the Lord Justices who had to come all the way from Dublin. They did so and placed their signatures upon the treaty. The Irish were guaranteed all the rights of citizens and were to be, "secure from any and all disturbances at the hands of the English".

The Treaty of Limerick was signed in 1691, although it was not approved by the English parliament until 1697, and then, in a seriously altered form. Irish officers and soldiers were given the choice of staying in Ireland, swearing an oath of allegiance to William, and living in peace; or, they would be allowed to leave the country. Over ninety-five percent elected to leave the country. This has come to be known historically as the "Flight of the Wild Geese". Many of these Irish officers and soldiers went on to distinguish themselves in armies and conflicts around the world.

The "faith and honour" of the British Crown were pledged to the Irish in the "Treaty of Limerick", yet within three years of its signing, the harshest of all Penal Laws and the most fervent of all persecutions against Catholics were begun in Ireland. The English Protestant clergy screamed from their pulpits about the "sins" of keeping faith with, and/or promises to, the Papists.

The Eighteenth Century

The Penal Laws enacted following the Williamite Wars were the harshest and most brutal of any in recorded history. Furthermore they were quite unique in the fact that they were not directed at a religious minority, such as, for example, the Huguenots in France; but they were directed at the overwhelming majority of the population. Also, the aim was not to convert or force into exile the targets of their persecution, but to reduce the population to a status of impotent subservience. Every effort was made to disallow nine-tenths of the population to better themselves socially, economically, or in any other way.

The fervent brutality became even worse after the German Hanoverians, beginning with George I, ascended to the English throne in 1714. To demonstrate the scope and intent of these penal laws—between 1695 and 1720, laws were enacted forbidding the Irish Catholics from any of the following:

> They were to own no gun, sword, knife, nor any weaponry.
> They were excluded from their country's parliament.
> They were excluded from their country's military.
> They could hold no government position, nor job.
> They could not enter the legal profession.
> They could not teach nor maintain schools.
> They could not send children abroad to be educated.
> They could not own nor buy land.
> They were prohibited from receiving land as a gift.
> They were forbidden to join any profession.
> They could not own a horse worth more than five pounds.

They were forbidden from voting.
Catholics were forbidden from inheriting from Protestants.
They were not allowed to engage in commerce (major factor).
They could not be the guardian of, nor foster, a child.
They could make no profit from their land exceeding 30% of rent.
Upon the death of parents, no child could be left with Catholics.
They could not attend any Catholic worship services.
Priests and catholic clergy were outlawed under penalty of death.

If an unhappy or unfaithful wife would become Protestant,
she would then receive all of the family property.
They were forbidden from speaking the Irish language.
They could not listen to Irish music.
They could engage in no Irish customs.

These laws were designed to accomplish cultural genocide, and to eliminate Roman Catholics from Ireland; and, in effect by their wording ignored, or presupposed, that no such people even existed. What extreme arrogance! Furthermore, any magistrate could visit the house of any Irish Catholic, at any hour of the day or night, for the purpose of searching for weapons. One need only imagine the horrendous stories that came from these situations.

Catholic clergy were especially targeted. They were outlawed, and if anyone came upon one, he was obligated to kill him immediately. They held mass, as well as educational classes, far out into the wilds, with numerous sentries posted in an attempt to insure their safety. These became known as "hedge schools" or "hedge meetings", because the teachers and students often hid behind, or among, the hedges. Teachers and Clergy had to dress in rags and act stupid, and were still quite often discovered, usually betrayed by a paid informer, perhaps someone desperately needing the money to feed his or her family. If groups were discovered worshipping on the mountainside, most often the entire group was slaughtered.

To insure that the Penal Laws were being enforced, the various counties had to issue annual "Returns" stating how many Catholics had been arrested, and the numbers currently being held in jails and prisons. These have been preserved in the official state records and cast an interesting perspective upon the Penal Laws. These laws were enforced all the way to the end of the Eighteenth Century, and led in part to the development of the "Volunteer" movement.

England attempted to wipe out Irish trade and industry with the same enthusiasm with which they sought to wipe out Catholicism. The Irish had been international traders and artisans for many centuries, with documented dealings going as far back as the Phoenicians. They were known throughout the world for their excellent art, craftsmanship, and weaving.

The woolen industry was booming at the time of the English occupation, and the English then mandated that the Irish could export woolen products to nowhere except England, and then at a very low price. They were still permitted however to produce and export hemp and linen. When the Irish developed these commodities into a profit-producing mode, these were then also outlawed by England. The Irish next turned to cattle and sheep. These were soon outlawed. Next came the production of cheese and butter (still considered among the finest in the world), and the English were annoyed at having to amend the laws to include these.

The Irish then began exporting butchered meat. This became outlawed. Next came the extremely fine glass industry (the Irish still produce arguably the world's finest crystal)–this was then outlawed. Next came fishing and fisheries, and these were also forbidden from exportation–all under the pretense that the enemies of Britain were in no way to be supplied with these. Oh yes, I forgot about the silk industry that came to prominence in the middle of the Eighteenth Century, exportation of silk was again forbidden. Many historians argue that these measures were the most devastating of all to the Irish people, keeping them subservient and without an avenue to freedom for several generations. Many of these industries haven't recovered to this very day, basically because of the loss of market share.

It was inevitable that this sort of oppression would eventually again lead to an Irish Nationalist, or Republican-type, movement. The Irish were also well aware of the events taking place in America. In April of 1778, the American John Paul Jones sailed into Belfast Harbor and in broad daylight sank a British Man-of-war ship. Shortly thereafter, the first corps of "Irish Volunteers" was formed in Belfast.

Theobald Wolfe Tone and the United Irishmen:

The Irish had been dealing with the English for quite some time now and had learned of their ways. The Irishmen were becoming wiser and more realistic; and, were beginning to realize that their only hope rested in knowledge, unity, and arming themselves against the English invaders and oppressors. By 1780, the "Irish Volunteers" numbered over 100,000 armed and disciplined men. They were led and trained by officers that had learned their trade in some of the finest armies of Europe.

The American experience and the redress of the intolerable evils, especially those involving the trade embargoes, suffered by the Irish at the hands of the English soon became the main topics of both political and parlor discussions. The first step proposed in meetings called by the Volunteers was a movement calling for the non-importation, or boycotting, of English goods. The Irish would only eat, wear, and utilize goods produced in Ireland. The Volunteers were to see that the embargo was obeyed, warning merchants and shopkeepers of possible severe consequences for not doing so. This was a bold and effective measure.

In October 1779, a bill was introduced into the Irish Parliament calling for "Free Trade" for Ireland, allowing Ireland to import and export whatever products she so desired. In front of Trinity College, Napper Tandy had located his Irish Volunteers and their artillery cannons pointed at the Parliament Building, along with a placard that read "Free Trade or _____". Within a couple of weeks the embargo of, and exportation restrictions placed on, Irish goods were removed.

All appeared as if it was going well, but the truth of the matter was that the Irish Parliament was still under the restrictions imposed by the Poynings Act, and was in fact a puppet of the English parliament. On the nineteenth of October 1781, Cornwallis surrendered to the Americans at Yorktown, and the English parliament became quite fearful that the Irish would attempt to follow suit and seek independence. They began planning methods to which Ireland would be permanently tied to England, while at the same time the Volunteers were planning ways to severe this relationship.

I've mentioned previously the Poynings Act, which stated that the Irish Parliament could only deal with laws and legislation that the English parliament directed it to address or consider. In addition to this act, there was also the "Declaratory Act", also known as the "Sixth Act of George I", penned in 1719. This Act declared that the king of England also had the "full power and authority to make laws and statutes of sufficient force and validity to bind the people and the Kingdom of Ireland." Following the events in America, there was a bill rushed through the English Parliament repealing the Declaratory Act in 1782, with the announcement made shortly thereafter in the Irish Parliament.

There was a young counselor, or solicitor, by the name of Theobald Wolfe Tone who spent as much time as possible setting in the gallery in the Irish House of Commons. He was the first to write about the fact that these laws binding the Irish Parliament, as well as the connection with England, were at the root of the Irish people's problems. In 1790, he wrote, "That the influence of England was the radical vice of our Government, and that Ireland would never either be free, prosperous, or happy, until she was independent, and that independence was unattainable whilst the connection with England existed". England wanted it to appear through the repeal of the Declaratory Act that Ireland had been given its freedom, but Tone and others recognized that this was not the case.

Tone pointed to three main defects in this "independence". First, was the clause in the Constitution of 1782, that this "Irish Independence", "united Britain and Ireland under one Sovereign". It then further stated that this "independence", "annexed the crown of Ireland inseparably to the crown of Great Britain". Secondly, he noted that over three-quarters of the Irish population had no representation in this "Irish Parliament". Catholics, who made up over three-fourths of the Irish population, could neither sit in, nor vote for a member of this Parliament. And thirdly, that this Irish Parliament, even as an instrument of the Protestant minority, was totally inept, corrupt, and unrepresentative of Irish interests.

One day while viewing the follies of the Irish House of Commons, Tone met a young soldier, Captain Thomas Russell, and a lifelong friend-ship ensued. These two, and eventually several other like-minded individ-uals, began meeting at Tone's home in Irishtown and discussing such topics as the French and American revolutions, and the current oppressed, enslaved, and outcast conditions of both the Irish Catholics, and the Presbyterian Dissenters. Tone's group saw a need to unite these two fac-tions, as both were severely disenfranchised.

Tone then wrote a pamphlet entitled, "An Argument On Behalf of the Catholics of Ireland" and sent it to the Presbyterian Dissenters. He signed it "A Northern Whig", however his authorship was never really a secret, and in it he outlined the fact that these two groups had "one common interest and one common enemy". Out of this was formed the idea of a political action party of united Irishmen; and, on the Eighteenth of October, 1791, the first general meeting of the "United Irishmen" was held. Three resolutions were passed:

1) The weight of English influence in the Government of Ireland was so great that it required a cordial union among all the people of Ireland in order to maintain that balance which is essential to the preservation of all individuals' liberties, and the extension, growth and preservation of commerce.

2) The sole constitutional avenue by which this English influence may be opposed is by initiating complete and radical reform measures

regarding the methods of elected representation of those serving in the Irish Parliament.

3) That no reform is just nor proper that does not include Irishmen of every religious persuasion.

The United Irishmen were first founded in Belfast, but within a year there was a branch started in Dublin also. A prominent figure in this group was Napper Tandy, the fellow who had earlier trained his cannons on the House of Parliament. In early 1792, the newspaper, *The Northern Star*, under the editorship of Samuel Neilson, was founded to expound the views of the United Irishmen.

Eventually, England would employ every tactic imaginable to crush the United Irishmen. Laws known as the "Convention Acts" were passed that forbade Irishmen from holding or attending any public meetings. Police and magistrates were allowed to invade and smash to pieces any house, office, or newspaper that was suspected of having United Irishmen sympathies. At this time also, in 1795, the Orange Order was formed—an extremely secretive, violent, and bigoted organization whose main goal was to crush the United Irishmen, and intimidate these fair-minded individuals whose only wish was to include all Irishmen in a positive-minded effort to better Ireland. They claimed responsibility for driving every Catholic out of County Armagh, where the organization originated, almost exclusively through the use of intimidation and violence. Catholic churches were burned and the violence soon spread to counties Down, Derry, Antrim and Tyrone. This only drove people to more actively embrace the United Irishmen, and their spin-off group, The Defenders, who were organized to counter the efforts of the Orange Order.

Following approximately four years of purely constitutional efforts, the United Irishmen remodeled themselves along military lines, realizing this was the only way Ireland could defend herself sufficiently and achieve any sort of freedom. Looking again to the examples of France and America, Tone visited both these in an effort to secure their assistance. In 1796,

Tone had convinced the French to assist and an expedition to free Ireland was initiated. It was to land at Bantry Bay in the winter of 1796, but at the appointed time, the weather was so bad that the French fleet was unable to land and hence returned to France.

Following the failure of the Bantry Bay expedition, more and more people believed that the United Irishmen should rise up on their own and not rely on foreign aid. Hence, the "Rising of 1798" was organized. The English government became aware of this action and initiated an elaborate campaign of paid informers that were to infiltrate as deeply as possible the inner workings of the United Irishmen. Tone was back in France and had received a commitment of limited French aid. The informers learned just enough to identify the leaders of the Rising and their tentative plans, and just before the planned Rising, many of the leaders were arrested and killed, throwing a great deal of the plan into disarray. The small French fleet, including also Wolfe Tone, was surrounded and captured. Tone was dressed in a French officer's uniform and was extremely proficient in the French language. At first he was not detected, but then was recognized by a British officer who had attended Trinity College with Theobald, and he was taken prisoner. Wolfe Tone was given the sentence to be hung as a traitor. He requested to be executed as a soldier by firing squad, but when this was denied, he took his own life and died on the Nineteenth of November 1798.

The British themselves realized that the focus of much of the Irish discontent was the extremely incapable and corrupt "Irish" Parliament. To alleviate this problem England sought to devise a method of bringing Ireland directly under the control of the English parliament. William Pitt the Younger had become the Tory Prime Minister in 1783, and he was convinced that this was absolutely necessary to avoid further rebellion in Ireland. This they decided would be done through an "Act of Union". They knew they couldn't just thrust such a thing upon the Irish–they had to make it appear that the Irish wanted this union. The English then devised one of the most elaborate schemes of bribery, intimidation, and extortion the world has ever seen. They needed signatures–on petitions that favored the political union of Ireland and England.

They had learned previously that certain of the extremely poor and hungry people could be bribed. These were immediately paid for their signatures. Next, it became a requirement to sign the petition as a prerequisite to holding any government job or position; and, not only must you sign the petition, but so must all your relatives–for three generations. All avenues of government patronage were employed to secure signatures. The English clergy became involved and preached from their pulpits about the necessity of signing the petition. Of course the Orange Order was still active in the areas of violence and intimidation. Those brave enough to stand up for their independence and their rights, were abused and persecuted in extremely harsh ways, both publicly and privately.

In parliament session after parliament session the Act of Union was introduced and defeated. The English government then reapportioned legislative districts and actually paid these districts to send the desired candidates to parliament. Finally, by August of 1800, enough votes were gathered to pass the Act of Union. It took effect on 1 January 1801, and united Ireland and England into "The United Kingdom of Great Britain and Ireland". Historians have claimed that in excess of 8000 pounds was paid for each vote, and of all the votes cast for the Act of Union (162), only seven were not paid a bribe. Also, out of the over three hundred members of parliament, it is believed that possibly only seventy-two were legitimately elected. It has also been stated that the Act of Union received about as much respect for the "honour" of England on the world stage as did the Treaty of Limerick. Not many European countries cared for England at this particular time and the country was becoming more and more isolated on the world scene.

Over the next few years several attempts were made to again unite the Irishmen towards the cause of independence. Possibly among the most notable were the efforts of Robert Emmet, who united several factions of Irishmen and also again secured the promises of France to assist. The

Rising was planned for 23 July 1803. The French never showed up. It seems Napoleon Bonaparte was only using the Irish, their hopes, and his promises to them, as pawns in his much larger scheme. Robert Emmet's brother, Thomas Addis Emmet, declared that, "Bonaparte was the worst enemy Ireland ever had"(MacManus, 1990). Robert Emmet was publicly beheaded in front of Dublin Castle on the twentieth of December 1803.

Watching all this was a young solicitor (lawyer) by the name of Daniel O'Connell who was born in County Kerry in 1775. His uncle Daniel had been one of the "Wild Geese". In young Daniel's youth he had watched John Paul Jones chasing the British ships around the seas of Ireland. When the heavily oppressed Catholics of the early Nineteenth Century were being told that their best course of action was that of "dignified silence", the young O'Connell urged agitation.

The Nineteenth Century

Discussed in the last section were such figures as Theobald Wolfe Tone, Robert Emmet, Thomas Emmet and Napper Tandy. We watched the progression from the Irish Volunteers and Defenders to the United Irishmen, and then on to the development of the Catholic Committee. Finally it was noted that a young solicitor by the name of Daniel O'Connell had been watching all this transpire. I believe we mentioned that Daniel O'Connell was born in County Kerry in 1775, in Cahircaveen near the southwest coast to be more specific.

His family had made a rather substantial fortune in the smuggling business. We discussed the very stringent and oppressive restrictions the English had placed on Irish imports and exports. The O'Connells imported a great many items that were either unavailable or prohibitively expensive, such as continental foodstuffs, wine, European cloth; and, they lived in the near perfect location, on the sea, surrounded by mountain ranges that pretty much isolated them from the remainder of Ireland. Daniel's uncle, also named Daniel, was one of the "wild geese" and helped organize shipments from abroad.

Daniel first broke onto the national scene in 1808, at the age of thirty-three years, when he became the spokesman for the more militant faction of the Catholic Committee, demanding equal rights for Catholics. The British Parliament had agreed to remove a few minor restrictions on Catholics and O'Connell claimed the action was not near the scope that it should be; and, also the legislation contained a clause that allowed the English to review all correspondence and interactions between Rome and the Irish Catholic Church. O'Connell went to Pope Pius VII himself and called for Catholic action and agitation. At that time the Catholic hierarchy, represented by the "Catholic Board", had become quite demure and conciliatory, following years of terror and brutality. But, Ireland had now found a new leader and by 1811, the Catholic Board was so bold and militant that the English outlawed it. A few years later he began an association with the United Irishmen in Dublin and further developed his Nationalist sentiments.

He was thrust into the position of National Hero basically as the result of two further incidents: one was the trial of John Magee in 1813, and the second was his duel with a retired English naval officer and Orangeman by the name of D'Esterre.

In 1813, a newspaper known as *The Evening Star*, which was owned by Magee, wrote the truth about the murder and oppression being perpetuated by such English agents as Westmoreland, Camden, and Cornwallis. The Government immediately brought charges against Magee and he employed O'Connell as his solicitor. The Government Attorney General, an avid Irish-hating Orangeman by the name of Saurin, decided to handle the prosecution himself. The entire jury was composed of Orangemen, as was the Lord Chief Justice.

O'Connell saw that his client had basically no chance, so he lashed into a scathing attack of this mockery of justice; and, of the British system of Government. He taunted and scoffed at the Lord Chief Justice, the Prosecutor, and the jury calling them hypocrites and liars. This speech was considered his best of over hundreds that he would eventually deliver, and was published in its entirety the next day in Dublin, in a newspaper called *The Post*, along with various political cartoons–the most famous of which depicted Saurin as a beaten and profusely sweating pig.

His actions infuriated the English who actually tried to have him removed from the practice of Law. He simply ignored them and embraced the overwhelming gratitude of the Irish people. If anything could have possibly further endeared "The Counsellor", as he was now affectionately being called, to the hearts of the Irish people, it was certainly his duel with

D'Esterre–an exceptional pistol shot who had been recruited by the Orangemen to challenge O'Connell.

D'Esterre first sent word to O'Connell, while Daniel was arguing a case in the Four Courts, that D'Esterre was planning to pummel him when he exited the building and would be waiting for him on Grafton Street. Well when Dan came out he grabbed a blackthorn walking stick and headed for Grafton Street. By the time he arrived at the appointed location, a crowd of thousands had gathered and D'Esterre hurriedly rolled up his horse-whip and snuck out the rear door of a beauty parlor.

D'Esterre next challenged O'Connell to a pistol duel, of which D'Esterre was considered an expert. They agreed on a secret location in County Kildare to escape the throngs, and were to be accompanied by only a few friends and a surgeon. Well, somehow the word leaked out and by the time they reached the appointed location, there was a substantial crowd already gathered. D'Esterre showed up half-an-hour late. The men faced off and at the drop of the handkerchief D'Esterre stepped to one side in an attempt to confuse O'Connell as both shots rang out. D'Esterre fell mortally wounded, and Dan O'Connell was the undisputed leader of the Irish people.

O'Connell, as well as having incorporated Nationalist sentiments, was still somewhat awed by the symbolism of the Royal throne; and, had in reality hoped that someday all could live in harmony and peace–perhaps something of an Idealist if you will. He had even proposed a "Royal Georgian Club", where English and Irish could mingle at least six times per year and march together wearing rosettes of royal blue, the combination of their green and orange. He even at one time, following the Irish visit of George IV in 1821, proposed the construction of an Irish royal residence, offering to contribute twenty pounds per year.

George IV did in fact make some concessions, and perhaps held a dear spot in his heart for Ireland, as he spoke fondly of Ireland for some time after returning from that visit. O'Connell had the Irish people's mixed support for his policies of planned cooperation. In 1821, the English

House of Commons passed the Catholic Relief Bill, which would have permitted Catholics to hold many government positions and would have made Catholics eligible for parliament; but, it also contained one unacceptable clause–that being that the Catholic Bishops must swear an oath of allegiance to the Royal Crown.

O'Connell had to basically start over. He found it a particularly good time for agitation, and also founded a new Catholic Association, organized by parishes. The churches and the priests then became the natural unifying points and leaders respectively. A dues or fee of one pence (penny) per month was charged of all members, and this was collected at the chapel's door on the first Sunday of each month. This gave the Catholic Association an income of over one-thousand pounds per week, and in a relatively short time the entire country was more organized, and possibly more unified, than it had ever been before.

The people were again watching world affairs and saw Simon Bolivar securing Independence for South America–Ireland even sent him a brigade to assist, led by Morgan O'Connell, Daniel's son. They also saw the Greeks gaining their Independence from the Turks. These events inspired, motivated, and emboldened the Irish populace to an attitude perceived as dangerous by the British government. They suppressed the Catholic Association, declaring it was not recognized in the eyes of the law.

In 1825, a compromise was penned, called the "Emancipation Bill". One provision of the bill was that the Catholic clergy was to be paid by the British government. This, the British hoped, would inspire the loyalty of both the clergy and the Irish people. The bill passed the House of Commons and would probably have passed the House of Lords, but the king's brother, the Duke of York, began an angry and threatening campaign outlining the evils of the bill. The bill was ultimately dismissed from the House of Lords, with the House of Lords itself being dissolved in a frenzy of confusion, and a new anti-Catholic cloud arose in the country of England.

O'Connell had to start anew and founded the "New Catholic Association", to replace the outlawed "Catholic Association". It was organized "for the purpose of public and private charity and such other purposes as are not forbidden by the statute of George IV". By this simple name change and the changing of the statement of purposes to things that were not recently outlawed in the "Suppression Act", O'Connell's movement never lost momentum. It in fact gained momentum, and solidarity, fed again by the extreme anti-Catholic sentiment now sweeping through Britain.

In 1826, the results of the Parliamentary elections in Britain were overwhelmingly in favor of the conservative "anti-popery" movement. In Ireland, they were the exact opposite, overwhelmingly dominated by the Catholics. In 1828, a Parliamentary vacancy came up from the region of Clare. The people convinced Daniel O'Connell to run. (Remember, no Catholic was permitted to hold a seat in parliament.) This election, from all accounts was quite some spectacle. The Landowners were intimidating and threatening their tenants, and the priests were urging the people to vote from their hearts for the first time in their lives. Everyone was in the streets with signs, brass bands, and singing choruses. The election voting lasted for one week, Monday through Saturday, and everyday tens of thousands were in the streets. In the end, O'Connell won by a margin of two-to-one. Sir Robert Peel at first declared that he could never consent to a Roman Catholic setting in the House of Commons; but, within a few months when he realized that five-sixths of Britain's military was trying to keep peace in Ireland, he declared, "I consider such a state of things much worse than rebellion".

In 1829, the "Emancipation Bill" was introduced to parliament. It narrowly passed over fierce opposition. Lord Wellington apologized for bringing it to the House of Lords, stating only that it was less evil than war. At first the king refused to sign it, ranting and threatening just about everyone. Peel and Wellington resigned, and the king was unable to find people willing to serve in a new ministry. He then recalled Peel and

Wellington, signed the Bill in a rage, and throwing the pen upon the ground, jumped up and down on it screaming that he had "betrayed God and the English people". In theory, Catholics could now hold government positions and were entitled to the same rights as others; but, as we shall see, they would still suffer from the same previously developed prejudices for many generations, in parts of Ireland yet up until this very day.

Following Emancipation, O'Connell's popularity grew even more renowned. He was now considered one of the greatest men in Europe, and certainly the greatest in Ireland's history. He then gave up his law practice and took up the causes of the people. This is when the famous "Tribute" was begun. It was a donation given by the people of Ireland for the support of Daniel O'Connell. It ranged from ten thousand to fifty thousand pounds per year, each of which was well earned and well spent according to all published accounts.

After Emancipation had been won, the next major step was to repeal the Act of Union. O'Connell started a weekly "repeal breakfast" and proclaimed that if these were suppressed, he would then initiate Repeal Lunches, Repeal Dinners, Repeal Suppers, and Repeal Feasts. He then began no less than eight organizations advocating repeal of the Act of Union, each of these taking the place of its outlawed predecessor. These included the General Association for Ireland, A Body of Persons, A Party Meeting for Dinner, the Repeal Association, the Irish Society for Legal and Legislative Relief, the Anti-Union Association, the Association of Irish Volunteers for Repeal of the Union, and the Association of Subscribers to the Parliamentary Intelligence Office. He so exhausted and infuriated the British government that they finally arrested him. He argued the court case himself until the law charging him had expired, the "Act for Suppression of Illegal Societies".

He then somewhat backed off from the repeal effort and led the fight for the removal of tithes. The protestant Church of England and its counterpart in Ireland, the Church of Ireland, were supported by mandatory tithes that all persons must pay, amounting to one-tenth of their income.

The Irish Catholics hated this law that made them pay for an extremely wealthy church that didn't even service one-tenth of the population, and none of them, while these same Irish people often didn't even have enough food to eat. In many of the more Catholic regions, often protestant ministers were receiving an enormous income and church fund for preaching to no one other than their family.

Government process-servers came around to collect the tithes. People began not paying, so the process-servers then employed armed guards, who would confiscate their cattle or whatever they could extract of value. In County Wexford during the summer of 1830, seventeen Irish farmers were killed by these "government workers", while the farmers were trying to retrieve their cattle that had been seized. In November of that year, eighteen process-servers and guards were killed while trying to confiscate cattle in County Kilkenny. The "Tithe War" was escalating. Twenty-five men were put on trial in Kilkenny and Daniel O'Connell went to defend them. He destroyed the government's case against them and the men were set free. The Tithe War raged on with the government trying everything to accomplish the impossible task. Finally, in 1838, the tithe was reduced by one-fourth and shifted to the responsibility of the landlords. Most of them then attempted to raise the rents, but this didn't work as the farmers refused to pay and the landlords either needed the workers; or, would evict the workers only to find that no one else would work for them.

Following the Tithe War, O'Connell again turned his attention toward repeal of the Act of Union. In 1841, there was elected for the first time in history a Nationalist Corporation to oversee the affairs of Dublin, replacing the Orangemen-dominated Dublin Corporation. To the joy of over five-sixths of Ireland, Daniel O'Connell was elected the first Nationalist Lord Mayor. In his acceptance speech he stated that he would be fair and non-political in all dealings, but would be a "Repealer to my last breath". O'Connell had been very disappointed by the fact that the Reform Act of 1832, had not restored the forty-shilling freehold vote. By 1840, it was clear that the Whig-led government, under Lord Melbourne, that

O'Connell had supported and helped put in power, was going to give way to the much less sympathetic Tory government, led by Sir Robert Peel. "The Liberator", as O'Connell was now called, became more aggressive and decided to more vigorously press the repeal issue.

In 1840, he formed the National Repeal Association, mentioned previously. He declared 1843 "Repeal Year" and forty "Monster Meetings" were then scheduled throughout the country. The London Times officially reported that a million people attended the meeting held on the Hill of Tara, but other reports indicated there were far more, perhaps even twice that number. The Association, and deep passion for the repeal of the Act of Union, grew and Dan called for a general meeting to be held on 8 October 1843, at Clontarf, the place of Brian Boru's great victory. Hundreds of thousands, possibly even millions, were expected to attend. The government got nervous, and banned the meeting, sending in five regiments of soldiers with dozens of cannons and full artillery. O'Connell, who really always believed in constitutional solutions, called for calm and gave way. He told his Repealers that, "nothing would justify his permitting vast masses of unarmed men to be mowed down".

The next morning, the government arrested O'Connell, his son John, several leaders of the movement, including two priests, and the editors of three Nationalist papers, *The Freeman's Journal, The Pilot,* and *The Nation.* They were charged with "conspiring to change the constitution by illegal methods", and were tried by a court exclusively comprised of Orangemen. No Catholic was permitted to serve in any capacity. O'Connell was sentenced to one year in prison, given a two-thousand pound fine, and was given another seven years of probation during which time he could organize no associations. After he was released from jail, he was never the same and had lost much of the fire that had characterized his younger days.

During O'Connell's time in prison, the Repeal movement also lost much of its fire; and, in the following year, 1845, the first potato blight hit- initiating the Great Famine, or more accurately now called the Great Hunger, as these years saw substantial exports of Irish-grown crops by the wealthy landlords. The Irish people were starving and had far more on their minds than Repeal. O'Connell died on 15 May, 1847.

While O'Connell was in jail, a new movement was however taking shape that should be here mentioned for their later influence. It was formed by a group of journalists who became known as "Young Ireland". One was John Mitchel, who believed in armed rebellion and founded a journal called the *United Irishman*; and, I believe was also an ancestor of the American Legislator, John Mitchell, who helped negotiate the current "Belfast Agreement". They kept the fight alive, but as previously mentioned the Great Hunger prohibited the people from having much time for organization and unification. Mitchel and most of the leaders were arrested in 1848, after the Young Irelanders had moved from agitation to armed rebellion, initiating a skirmish at Ballingarry in County Tipperary. Some of them fled to America and many were shipped to the Australian island of Tasmania (Van Diemen's Land). Mitchel escaped from the British jail in Australia and went to America, where he published his influential *Jail Journal*.

The Great Hunger actually lasted into the winter of 1849-1850. In 1845, Ireland's population was over eight million, and by 1850, over one million had died, and another million to a million-and-a-half had emigrated. The long-term effects of the Great Famine were immense, and in some respects are felt to this very day. The upward social mobility of the population was halted, the traditional hostility between tenants and landlords was magnified as many landlords ignored the plight of the people, and a greater hostility or resentment towards the British government developed as they were seen as taking inadequate measures to relieve the suffering. An enduring bitterness developed among the Irish people who could not escape the visions of people starving to death while livestock and grain were being exported from Ireland, often under military guard.

The ideals of the "Young Ireland" movement had been preserved in the hearts of the refugees. Some had settled in France and were inspired by the passionate revolutionary ideals permeating that society. Others had gone to America and joined forces with the large Irish populations of the eastern coast, especially New York–mostly people who had fled the famine. A fellow named James Stephens organized these and then covertly returned to Ireland and on St. Patrick's Day, 1858, officially founded a "secret" society known as the "Fenian Brotherhood" (Fenian being derived from Finn McCool's legendary band of warriors called the "fian"). It was to become known in Ireland as the "Irish Republican Brotherhood", and this name was officially adopted after a reorganization of the Republican movement in 1873.

The Fenian Brotherhood was also formalized in America on St. Patrick's Day, 1858, and those in exile there were to tap America's vast resources to assist with funds and weaponry. The Fenians saw no hope outside of armed revolution, and for this were denounced by the Catholic Church. Stephens then began publishing a newspaper called *The Irish People* in 1863, and used the American Civil War as an example and training ground for the study of maneuvers, strategy, and tactics. The membership oath for these two organizations was drafted by Thomas Clarke Luby and was really quite simple, "I _____ _____, in the presence of the Almighty God, do solemnly swear allegiance to the Irish Republic, now virtually established, and that I will do my very utmost at every risk, while life lasts, to defend its independence and integrity; and, finally, that I will yield implicit obedience in all things, not contrary to the laws of God, to the commands of my superior officers. So help me God, Amen."(Kenny, 1994)

Stephens was arrested in November of 1865, along with several other Fenian leaders and locked under maximum security in Richmond Jail, Dublin. One morning he was mysteriously gone, his jail cell standing wide open. This made sensational headlines throughout Europe. The British were infuriated and for almost three weeks continuously searched every corner of Dublin to no avail. All of a sudden one day a magnificent carriage and four horses pulled up to a house in Dublin, Stephens got in and paraded through the streets of Dublin before boarding a ship bound for France. All the coachmen were armed Fenians, and before a large enough police force could be summoned, Stephens was sailing for France. A few months later he was back in America.

The Fenians of Ireland by 1865 numbered over 100,000, and were also active among the Irish population in England, and in September of 1867, they attempted to seize Chester Castle, a large arms depot. They were unsuccessful and five Fenians were captured. Three of these were executed (William Allen, Michael Larkin, and Michael O'Brien) following an escape attempt where a British guard was killed. The other two of the Fenians involved, Thomas Kelly and John McCafferty, successfully escaped. These executions only added fuel to the Fenian fire. The three executed became known as the "Manchester Martyrs".

Records indicate that the Fenians were perhaps strongest and most efficiently organized in America, were even sold quantities of arms by the American government, and were permitted to meet freely in America. One of their plans even called for the invasion of Canada, which was known in advance by the American government (this fact placed great strain on British-American relations for several years); and, was in fact initiated on 31 May 1866. The invasion was to be a three-pronged assault, launched from Vermont in the east, Buffalo in the central regions, and Chicago in the west. The Buffalo-based group was the only one really getting off the ground; and, General John O'Neill led a band of Fenians that captured the British Fort Erie. They next routed a Canadian army regiment at a place called Limestone Ridge on 2 June 1866. Public opinion then forced America to declare that they could not condone this, and no more Fenians would be permitted to cross the border; but those already there were allowed to return to America safely. O'Neill actually tried invading Canada on two more occasions, in 1870 and 1871, briefly capturing the Canadian town of Pembina, Manitoba, in 1871. This was basically the end of the Fenian movement in the United States, as it was being rapidly replaced by the "Clan na Gael" (the Irish Race), which would develop into the most enduring and effective of the American republican movements.

In 1869, the official Established Church of England, which only a few years before had been forced upon the people, was disestablished. In the following year, the first land act, The Land Act of 1870, was made law. British Prime Minister Gladstone later confessed that the actions of the Fenians had forced him to initiate both these measures.

Two issues pretty much dominated the 1870's and 1880's. These were namely "Home Rule" and "Land Reform"; and, they were generally inter-related. One of the best solicitors in Dublin was a Tory Member of Parliament for Trinity College by the name of Isaac Butt. He was retained to defend the Fenian prisoners in Dublin. He came to learn a great deal about the Fenian ideals; and, ironically became a major advocate for the cause of Irish Independence. He invented a new term, "Home Rule". A "Home Government Association" was formed (it was later renamed the "Home Rule League"). Its first meeting was held in a Dublin Hotel in 1870, and it passed a resolution stating, "The true remedy for the evils of Ireland is the establishment of an Irish Parliament with full control over our domestic affairs". The old demand for the repeal of the Act of Union was discarded, and the new demand was for "Home Rule", which by its very nature implied a much broader scope.

The next step involved organizing a new political party, but Butt was not really effective in leading this new party. His vision was slightly different than that of most Irishmen. He envisioned a federal system in which Ireland would also continue to send delegates to the English Parliament at Westminster. The man who sculpted the new party advocating Home Rule, from then on called the Irish Parliamentary Party, was a southern Irish protestant by the name of Charles Stewart Parnell. Parnell was not a great orator, but he was an efficient organizer, basing his actions on sound political judgments; and, he also possessed a rather commanding personal charisma. In 1877, Isaac Butt died and after the elections of 1880, Parnell took over sole leadership of the party. He was also President of the Irish National Land League, which had been created in October 1879.

The Land League was actually the brainchild of Michael Davitt, who had served over seven years in Dartmoor prison for his part in the Fenian raid on Chester Castle. The Land League sought what they called the "Three F's"–fair rent, fixed tenure, and the free sale of tenancy at a fair market value. Between 1870 and 1876, there were fourteen legislative efforts to amend the Land Laws, all being unsuccessful. The landlords were asking rents that the land could not produce, and in 1876, there were again crop failures that bordered on famine. A couple of the more abusive landlords were shot, including one named Lord Leitrim in Donegal, who supposedly asked exorbitant rents and then demanded the tenants' wives and daughters be given as payment.

The Land League developed a new strategy, if a landlord was abusive, or unfairly evicted a tenant, the League would not allow anyone else to occupy the land or do business with that particular landlord. The very first landlord to be effected was an English Captain named Charles Boycott, whose name has forever more been incorporated into our language. Boycott could not get his crops harvested from the fields, nor could he get his horses shod, nor his carriages repaired. He asked for British assistance. Eventually, fifty Orangemen from the north and two thousand British soldiers came to assist him. They had to walk fifteen miles in the rain from the train station, as no one would transport them. They then camped in his front yard. They had brought no provisions, because they reckoned if they were going to do his work, the Captain would supply their needs. They ate up all his cattle, pigs, turkeys, geese, chickens, and crops before leaving. Captain Boycott was far worse off when they left, than before they had arrived

The "Gladstone Land Act of 1881", finally guaranteed the "Three F's", over violent opposition in the House of Lords. It was something of a catch-22, however because if the tenants made any improvements whatsoever to their homes, then their rents could be raised (Landlords never made any improvements nor repairs). In October 1881, Parnell was arrested under the Coercion Act and imprisoned in Dublin's Kilmainham

Jail. When he was asked who would take his place, he remarked, "Captain Moonlight" (Groups of tenants who by night harassed abusive landlords were known as "Moonlighters"). The British government eventually realized that it better served their interests to have Parnell out of jail than in, and released him in May of 1882.

The "Irish National League" was formed in 1882, and placed its emphasis on Home Rule, rather than Land Reform. Parnell would have originally been content to accept for Ireland a subservient parliament, dealing exclusively with domestic affairs. In the election of 1885, however, Parnell's Irish Parliamentary Party won eighty-six seats in Parliament and held the balance of power between the Liberals, led by Gladstone, and the Conservatives, led by Lord Salisbury. Gladstone became Prime Minister with Parnell's support, and in April 1886, introduced his first "Home Rule Bill", which provided for both an Irish Parliament and an Irish Executive Branch. With ninety-three of the Liberals voting against the bill it was defeated by a count of 343 votes to 313 votes. The Conservatives then overwhelmingly won the next general election, with Parnell and Ireland already committed to the Liberal side.

In December 1889, Parnell was named as a co-respondent in a divorce action brought by an Irish Member of Parliament, Captain William O'Shea. Parnell offered no defense, and after the divorce he married Kitty O'Shea. This cost him the leadership of his party and he died in October, 1891, at forty-five years of age, worn out, somewhat socially disgraced, and embittered.

The Irish Parliamentary Party and its leadership floundered for several years, and when John Redmond announced in the British House of Commons in 1914, that Irish soldiers would fight for England in World War I, after Ireland had already declared neutrality, the party disappeared from existence forever in a final disgrace.

The Gaelic League, Sinn Fein, and The Easter Rising

In 1893, The Gaelic League was formed by Douglas Hyde and Eoin MacNeill. This came on the heels of the Gaelic Athletic Association, which had been organized only a few years earlier in 1884, and was having great success in renewing pride and interest in traditional Irish athletics, such as hurling, Gaelic football, etc. (Its primary founder was a very interesting fellow by the name of Major John MacBride, born in 1865 in Westport, County Mayo. He joined the Irish Republican Brotherhood in the 1880's, fought in the Boer War against the English, married the beautiful actress, and republican activist and organizer, Maud Gonne in 1903, fought in the G.P.O. in 1916, and was executed by the English on 5 May of that year.) The Gaelic League promoted the cultural aspects of traditional Ireland, especially the Irish language, art, literature, and drama. The writings and plays of W. B. Yeats, Lady Gregory, Standish O'Grady, and increasing numbers of other writers and scholars led to an incredible revival of Irish pride, identity, and nationalistic sentiment. The influence of the Gaelic League grew like wild fire.

In 1899, Arthur Griffith began publication of a magazine called the *United Irishman*, whose contributors included some of the most accomplished minds of the day—in the fields of drama, essay writing, political prose, and current research. In 1903, the Abbey Theatre was founded by William Butler Yeats and Lady Gregory, primarily to further call attention to nationalistic ideals. This too drew the most accomplished playwrights of the day, with a strong emphasis on Irish heritage and nationalism. It has been immensely popular ever since, winning numerous awards, and always producing the most interesting and relevant of plays.

A fervent nationalistic pride in all things "Irish" was rapidly developing. It is interesting to note that after centuries of serious attempts to unify the Irish people, it was finally coming about in the middle of the nineteenth century, primarily through the efforts of a variety of artistic and scholarly pursuits. Many scholars, including Professor Etienne Rynne of University College, Galway, have argued that a series of archaeological discoveries and the ensuing pride in these Irish antiquities, namely the Cross of Cong, The Tara Brooch, and the Ardagh Chalice (all found and presented to the Royal Irish Academy shortly before the formation of the Gaelic League), along with the great illuminated works such as The Book of Kells, The Book of Durrow, The Book of Armagh; and, the artistic, literary, and theatrical endeavors previously mentioned were the dominating factors in the fosterage of Irish Nationalism. It can be argued that this fact still holds true today.

In 1905, Arthur Griffith and his friends brought to Ireland a new political movement based on a national identity, and immediately calling for withdrawal of Ireland's representatives from Westminster, and the establishment of an Irish Parliament with complete control over the affairs of Ireland.

Mr. Griffith began publication of a new weekly newspaper, which in effect replaced the *United Irishman* and was more politically orientated. It was called *Sinn Fein* (Irish—meaning "ourselves alone"). In *Sinn Fein*, Arthur Griffith showed Ireland how she could proceed in the handling all of her own affairs, including everything from establishing international commerce, to the establishment of rail and highway systems, to the coinage and printing of all her own money (the monetary unit was to be called the "gael"). Shortly after the publication of the weekly, Sinn Fein became a strong nationalistic political movement, and then an official political party, that led the fight for Irish Independence. A new feeling of Irish pride, potential, and accomplishment was evident everywhere, and the electricity in the air told everyone that the time was now right to strike for independence.

A national mercantile marine was established to engage in commerce with the European continent, whose markets were much more lucrative for the Irish than were the English markets. For years the English merchants had been buying Irish products for unnaturally low prices, then immediately carrying them to the continent for resale, reaping huge profits in the process. Also a program of boycotting certain foreign products, to thus protect Irish industries, was put into practice as well. Arthur Griffith was a determined Nationalist and he refused to settle for anything falling short of that ultimate goal. He taught that nationalistic ideals were to be incorporated into every aspect of Irish life. And this began happening—in art, literature, drama, economics, industrial and social programs.

Arthur Griffith was also a patient man, carefully planning his strategy, while waiting for the perfect parliamentary moment, something similar to what Daniel O'Connell had tried to do. The highly emotional centenary celebrations of the 1798 Rebellion and the British problems associated with the outbreak of the Boer War both boosted Irish morale and the belief that the perfect moment was very near. It came with the beginning of World War I.

At this time Sinn Fein, and a second Nationalistic movement called the Physical Force Party (actually a revived Irish Republican Brotherhood through the energetic efforts of Thomas Clarke, who had just returned from exile in America) began sharing ideas. The Physical Force Party published a magazine called "Irish Freedom", which also printed the works of several of the outstanding thinkers of the day, among them one of the most remarkable, Padraig Pearse. They also quite effectively influenced public opinion through a series of gatherings known as the "Wolfe Tone Clubs". Fenianism and Republicanism again became the key words, and the Fenians adopted a motto written by Fintan Lalor, "Repeal not the Union, but the conquest". Sinn Fein somewhat took a back seat to the more forceful Physical Force Party, who knew the time was now right when, in August of 1914, England became occupied with World War I.

Weapons began to be secured by the smugglers. The Irish Volunteers were marching every Sunday on maneuvers, and on one occasion, 26 July, 1914, the Irish Volunteers marched from Dublin out to the coastal city of Howth and blatantly met a ship loaded with arms in broad daylight and unloaded it. The Volunteers then marched back to Dublin before dispersing, each with his new weapon and a quantity of ammunition. British soldiers had been assembled and marched to the outskirts of Dublin to find no one. On their way back to their barracks, the people began hooting and hollering at them and they fired two volleys into the crowd, killing four innocent people, and wounding approximately fifty more. All of Ireland was in shock, as was the all of Europe. The funerals were massive affairs, with hundreds of thousands attending. The Volunteers protected the crowd, presented the Tricolours, and fired a military salute over the graves. Everyone knew revolution was in the air.

Next, England wanted Ireland to send the Volunteers to fight for England as her involvement in the war deepened. Both the political leaders and the Volunteers rejected the offer, and chose instead to parade through College Green and around the Parliament Building, on St. Patrick's Day of 1915, flying the Irish Tricolours.

Two extremely strong and dynamic personalities then came to the forefront as insurrection became eminent. These were the aforementioned Padraig Pearse, whose powerful and passionate philosophically orientated writings presented the Irish cause in a near spiritual context; and, James Connolly, a socialist who founded the Irish Socialist Republican Party and believed in the Marxist doctrine of Social Revolution. In 1913, he organized a series of strikes by the workers and organized the Irish Citizen Army to protect the workers from the police. Both men believed that the English system of capitalistic commercialism was the most wicked and corrupt force that could be inflicted upon any nation, and saw it as the root cause of Ireland's problems.

Connolly was the most determined, telling several friends as early as 1914 that he would not let the "great war" end without striking a blow for

Irish freedom, and he stirred like sentiments as well throughout the country with the writings in his newspaper. During Lent preceding the Easter Rising, he wrote such passionate, treasonous, and revolutionary material that a citizen armed guard stood watch day and night over his printing presses at Liberty Hall, anticipating the government to raid the premises at any moment, and this action, most believed would initiate the great rebellion. A week before Easter, the Irish Tricolour was raised over Liberty Hall as if the Republic had already been declared and established.

A national organized insurrection to be led by the Volunteers was scheduled for Easter Sunday. It was to develop from the ordinary marching and parade maneuvers into armed rebellion. However, during the week preceding, a German ship named the "Aud", disguised as a Norwegian timber ship, was intercepted by the British carrying the over twenty-thousand rifles, millions of rounds of ammunition, machine guns, artillery, and explosives that were to supply the Volunteers. The German crew was forced to scuttle the ship. In a panic, Eoin MacNeill, chairman of the Volunteers, actually put an article in the newspapers on Saturday informing all Volunteers that, "Owing to the very critical position, all orders given to Irish Volunteers for tomorrow, Easter Sunday, are hereby rescinded, and no parades, marches, or other movements of Irish Volunteers will take place. Each individual Volunteer will obey this order strictly in every particular". (Macmanus, 1990)

To a startled nation, shortly after noon on Monday, 24 April 1916, the Irish Tricolour was raised above the General Post Office in Dublin and the Irish Republic was proclaimed. It seems the British had learned about the insurrection following the Aud incident, and then planned to arrest all the Irish political leaders and leaders of the Volunteers within the week. No sooner had this decision had been made by the British, than it was relayed to the Irish through secret informers. The Volunteer Council met on Easter and decided that it was basically "now or never", and organized the limited insurrection, doomed to failure, for the following day. The insurgents may have doubted the likelihood of their success, but they were confident that this blow, and likely loss of Irish blood, would be the determining factor in the gaining of Irish Independence; and, they were correct.

The men fought bravely and there is little doubt that if the Aud had not gone down, the Irish would have most likely won on the field of battle. On Monday, 24 April, 1916, the Dublin Volunteers, sporting their weapons and one day's food rations occupied the General Post Office, the Four Courts, Liberty Hall, three train terminals, and several other minor locations surrounding the center of Dublin. They made two critical errors however–they did not attempt to occupy Trinity College or Dublin Castle. Trinity College was an ideal fortress with its massive walls and city-within-a-city resources. It also held a commanding position of the Parliament Building and the two main Dublin thoroughfares. The Volunteers thought there were large numbers of troops inside, but this was not the case. They also thought Dublin Castle was protected by far more British troops than was actually the case. If the Volunteers had captured these two strategic locations, the British would have been forced to back down.

Anyway, the Proclamation of the Irish Republic was published on thousands of leaflets and several giant placards. There was actually very little fighting on Monday, mostly just sporadic sniper fire. The British were totally unprepared, thinking the Irish had abandoned the project, and could not gather their soldiers quickly enough, as the Irish forces dug in and fortified their positions.

On Tuesday, a force of approximately 4500 British troops finally secured the Castle and began attacking the Irish strongholds. By Wednesday, Liberty Hall had been mostly destroyed and by Thursday, much of O'Connell Street was ablaze. The British forces then concentrated on destroying the rebels' headquarters, the General Post Office, over which the Republican Tricolour was still flying.

On Friday, an all-out bombardment had set basically the entire center of Dublin city ablaze. The numbers of non-combatant casualties were massive, and still rising. On Saturday, the General Post Office was set aflame, and the Republican insurgents had to flee out the back to a new location on Moore Street. Pearse sent a message, by way of a Red Cross Nurse, asking for terms. These were refused and at two o'clock in the afternoon, Pearse and the others surrendered unconditionally to the British commander, Sir John Maxwell.

Pearse then sent out word to the other Irish Commandants—Edward Daly at the Four Courts, Countess Markievicz, who had been driven from her position at Stephen's Green back to the College of Surgeons, Commandant Thomas McDonagh at Jacob's factory, DeValera at Boland's Mills (they had held the entire southern part of the city), and Commandant Eamonn Ceannt at the South Dublin Union, that they were told to lay down their arms.

A massive roundup of Irish Nationalists was then begun in all parts of the country. Many were sent to England and held in extremely unsanitary, rat-infested internment camps. Secret military trials were held and executions began. All those signing the Republican Proclamation, and fifteen in all, were shot before world outrage forced the British to discontinue the executions. Those shot were Padraig and William Pearse, James Connolly, Eamonn Ceannt, Michael O'Hanrahan, Sean MacDermott, Con Colbert, J.J. Houston, Thomas Ceannt (who was shot in County Cork), Joseph Mary Plunkett, Edward Daly, Michael Mallon, Thomas MacDonagh, Thomas Clarke, and John MacBride.

Towards Independence

As previously mentioned, Sinn Fein had pretty much given way during the Easter Rising to the more aggressive elements of the Physical Force Party, and as an organization Sinn Fein had not been officially involved. It now however seized upon the political opportunities and won a number of important elections in 1917. One of those winning a seat in parliament from the region of east Clare was Eamon de Valera, the only surviving commandant of the Easter Rising. By the end of 1917, he had replaced Arthur Griffith as the leader of Sinn Fein; and, in the general elections of 1918, Sinn Fein won seventy-three of the Irish seats in parliament and the Unionists won twenty-six.

The members of the Sinn Fein party refused to take their seats in Westminster, instead calling for an all-Irish parliament to meet in January 1919. They in fact did meet in Dublin in January and formed the Dail Eireann (Assembly of Ireland). The structure and particulars of the Dail Eireann had been finalized by late 1918 in preparation. Eamon de Valera had been arrested and jailed (as Sinn Fein and the Irish Volunteers had been declared illegal), but within a year he was released from Lincoln Jail and was elected president of the Dail Eireann in April of 1919. Shortly thereafter, he left for America to both raise funds and seek American support for "The Republic". He then also went to the Peace Conference at Versailles seeking support and recognition for The Republic.

It was becoming evident that Ireland and England were again heading towards war. The Irish Republican Army was now carrying out successful attacks against British troops and police. The leader of this activity was for the most part Michael Collins, who had fought in the General Post Office and was a master of intelligence, tactics and organization.

In March of 1920, the British reinforced their police, The Royal Irish Constabulary, with a force comprised of ex-soldiers and prisoners who carried the nickname of "Black and Tans", because they wore a uniform that was a combination of both the police and army uniforms. The Black and Tans were joined in Ireland, in August 1920 by the Auxiliaries, a group of ex-British army officers. Both of these groups engaged in hundreds of atrocities perpetrated against the Irish including torture, murder, burning, and rape. They were extremely undisciplined, brutal, and violent. In response to these, the Irish Republican Army's "Flying Columns" were formed and carried out a quite successful campaign of counter-attacks and ambushes against these forces. Many of the Large Houses of the more oppressive English landlords were burned down as well.

David Lloyd George, the British Prime Minister, then drafted the "Government of Ireland Act" which became law before the end of 1920. It provided for parliaments to be established in both Dublin and Ulster. "Northern Ireland" would consist of the six counties of Antrim, Armagh, Derry, Down, Fermanagh, and Tyrone. "Southern Ireland" would include the remaining twenty-six counties of Carlow, Cavan, Clare, Cork, Donegal, Dublin, Galway, Kerry, Kildare, Kilkenny, Laois, Leitrim, Limerick, Longford, Louth, Mayo, Meath, Monaghan, Offaly, Roscommon, Sligo, Tipperary, Waterford, Westmeath, Wexford, and Wicklow. In the "North" Unionists won forty of the fifty-two seats contested in the May 1921 elections. In the "South", Sinn Fein ran unopposed in 124 of the 128 seats. The remaining four seats were allocated to Unionists representing the University of Dublin (including Trinity College). These two governments were formed and the Irish War for Independence officially ended on 11 July 1921.

The treaty negotiations now began in London and lasted almost five months. The British delegation's leader was Prime Minister Lloyd George and the Irish delegation's leaders were Arthur Griffith and Michael Collins. Eamon de Valera had remained in Dublin, professing that this was his proper place. After much argument, and quite proficient and astute bargaining by the Irish delegation, the "Articles of Agreement for a Treaty between Great Britain and Ireland" was drawn up on 6 December 1921, and signed by the Irish delegation under the threat of the immediate resumption of war by a frustrated Lloyd George. Griffith and Collins had in fact secured substantial concessions in very important areas, such as defense, tariffs, taxation, commerce, policing, and nomenclature. Many of these they would not have predicted achieving originally. They thought they had done well, providing a giant stepping-stone from which further unity, independence, and self-government could be attained.

The Anglo-Irish Treaty provided that the new "Irish Free State" would govern itself, have dominion status (similar to that of Canada and Australia), that its members of parliament must swear an oath of allegiance to the British crown, and that Britain would be allowed to maintain certain naval bases in port cities. Northern Ireland was given the opportunity to "opt out" of this new Irish Free State if it so desired. The parliament in Belfast immediately took advantage of this clause. There was also a Boundary Commission established to "adjust the existing border in accordance to the wishes of the inhabitants, so far as may be compatible with economic and geographic conditions".

The Irish treaty delegates returned to Dublin, and the Dail Eireann became at once divided as to whether or not they should accept the terms of the treaty. Eamon de Valera was adamant about not swearing an oath of allegiance. Collins and Griffith believed they had secured the very best terms possible under the circumstances, and Michael Collins told the Dail the delegation, "had not received the ultimate freedom that all nations aspire and develop to, but had received the freedom to achieve it". Interestingly enough, partition of the island did not receive a great deal of attention in these debates. Most delegates seemed to believe this was a most temporary phenomenon as the Boundary Commission would surely take note of the wishes of the catholic majorities in counties Tyrone and Fermanagh. This would only leave four counties in Northern Ireland, and these could certainly never survive long as an independent political nor economic unit. The Dail Eireann voted by a count of sixty-four votes to fifty-seven votes on 7 January 1922, to accept the treaty. Eamon de Valera immediately resigned as president and was replaced by Arthur Griffith. On the sixteenth of January, a provisional government under the leadership of Michael Collins took possession of Dublin Castle, and the withdrawal of British troops and administrators was begun.

The two Irish factions, the pro-treaty "Free Staters" and the anti-treaty "Republicans", were still divided and adamantly opposed to each other's position. The strongest opposition to the treaty came from the south and west, from such counties as Cork, Tipperary, Kilkenny, and Wexford. In March and April of 1922, a group of anti-treaty dissidents calling themselves the "Irregulars" pledged allegiance to the Republic of 1916, and occupied the Four Courts, the Dublin Judicial Building, and a few other minor buildings, turning them into fortified positions. General elections were to be held on the sixteenth of June, so no immediate action was taken hoping the elections would provide a solution that would be honored by all. In the elections, only thirty-six seats out of one hundred and twenty-eight went to anti-treaty republicans. Approximately a week later the Irregulars occupying the Four Courts abducted a pro-treaty general, and Michael Collins ordered an attack on the building. On 26 June 1922, Free State troops opened fire on the Four Courts and the Irish Civil War had begun. Two days later, over one hundred Irregulars in the Four Courts surrendered.

On 12 August of that year, an extremely dismayed and exhausted Arthur Griffith died unexpectedly. Ten days later Michael Collins was killed in an ambush down in county Cork. During the next couple of months seventy-seven Republican prisoners were executed.

In September 1922, the new Dail Eireann met under heavy guard and began the process of writing a "Free State Constitution". William Cosgrave became president of the Dail, and Kevin O'Higgins became vice-president. From 1923 until 1927, the Republicans, and their party Fianna Fail, did not acknowledge this Dail Eireann, would not take the oath of allegiance, and would not take their seats in this Dail. During this period, with virtually no opposition party, the Dail Eireann established a new police force, a permanent army, put through several measures to aid Irish agriculture and industry, and implemented a plan to harness the River Shannon as a source of power.

In 1924, the Boundary Commission was organized as provided for by the treaty. Northern Ireland refused to appoint a delegate and swore not to yield one inch of ground. Eoin MacNeill, a Professor of Irish History, was the delegate appointed by the Free State and after attending several worthless meetings, resigned in disgust. No changes were ever made in the boundary. Eamon de Valera always criticized this partition, as did so many others, as a direct result of the 1921 treaty, and he began a political campaign to reverse this under the auspices of the political party Fianna Fail (Warriors, or Soldiers, of Destiny). Cosgrave's party was known as the Cumann na nGaedheal, later becoming simply the Fine Gael (Tribe of Gaels).

Over fierce opposition from the British, the Irish Free State succeeded in gaining a seat in the League of Nations, and established diplomatic relations with a number of other nations. Great progress was made during the Cosgrave administration, including the 1931 fight for the "Statute of Westminster", which recognized the unquestionable authority of each of Britain's several dominions to legislate for themselves in all sovereign matters.

In the general election of 1932, Fianna Fail won seventy-two out of one hundred and fifty-three seats, making it the majority party; and, with the support of the Labour Party, Eamon de Valera organized a new government. Over the next forty years, Fianna Fail would only be out of office for six short years (1948-1951 and 1954-1957). Eamon de Valera immediately abolished the oath of allegiance, and attempted to sever all other ties possible with Great Britain. De Valera always hesitated to declare, or even term, Ireland a Republic, because he believed she could never be so without her "Fourth Green Field" (Ulster, or the six counties of the

North). Instead, in 1937, he devised and had enacted a new "Constitution of Ireland", which in fact laid claim to all the island's national territory, but limited its jurisdiction to the twenty-six counties "pending the re-integration of the national territory". This provoked great anger and fury from both Britain and the Ulster unionists, whose parliament even then considered changing the North's name to the State, or Country, of Ulster.

Great Britain had initiated a number of severe economic reprisals following the beginning of de Valera's constitutional efforts and the dropping of the oath of fidelity. Fianna Fail then also employed protectionist economic policies eventually leading to a six-year economic war with Great Britain, ending in 1938. Trade was resumed slowly between the two after April 1938, when Prime Minister Chamberlain appeased the Irish by settling disputes regarding annuities and punitive debt; and, by surrendering the naval bases in Irish ports that had been allowed by the Anglo-Irish Treaty.

Fianna Fail had from the start ignored Britain's Governor General for Ireland, and after several unsuccessful rebuffs and protests, he resigned the position. A member of Fianna Fail assumed the post for a few years until the position was abolished in 1938.

Fianna Fail made passionate efforts to restore the Irish culture, history and pride. Irish was declared the "first official language" in the 1937 constitution, and along with British censorship, promoted an Irish-language counter-culture that produced some of the finest Irish writings of all time. (The English language would always have its place in Ireland, as many young Irish still looked to the glamour and possibilities of study and work abroad.)

The Irish Constitution, which took effect on 29 December 1937, called the "Bunreacht na hEireann", is rather unique in many principles. It declared Ireland is a free, independent, sovereign and democratic state with the people supplying all power and being the final arbiters on all matters. It recognized the family as the natural unit of society, and forbade divorce. It guaranteed all freedoms of conscience and religion. The community-held resources were to be distributed equally throughout society. And it acknowledged God as the ultimate source of all authority.

The constitution provides for a two-chamber parliament (Oireachtas), the Dail Eireann (members are called T.D.'s–Teachta Dalas, or Deputies) and the Seanad Eireann (members are called Senators) with a President of Ireland (Uachtaran na hEireann), elected by a direct vote of the people. I believe it was previously mentioned that the national territory was defined to include the thirty-two counties of Ireland, but until "re-integration", the jurisdiction of the parliament was limited to the twenty-six counties. The Republic was officially named "Eire" (Irish), and in English it was to be called Ireland.

Ireland remained neutral throughout World War II, although several of the combatants, including the United States, thought about invading the island. The United States had actually devised a plan to do so and came within a couple of weeks of implementing it, but I suppose this just never became necessary from a standpoint of strategic importance. Britain had a rather large naval base at Derry (now called Londonderry) in Northern Ireland, and from there protected her western coast without infringing upon the Free State. Reclaiming the old British naval bases had also been rather strongly considered by both the United States and Britain but was never acted upon. There is some evidence that Winston Churchill, the British Prime Minister, promised that if Ireland fought for the Allies, he would introduce legislation to unify Ireland. There is no indication that Eamon de Valera ever acted upon this information, probably for a variety of reasons.

Through this period, Fianna Fail, remained easily the largest political party, but several smaller political parties were organizing, such as the "Clann na Poblachta", or Republican Family. In 1948, many of these formed a coalition with Fine Gael and Labour; and, Fine Gael's John Costello became Taoiseach. Before the end of the year they had passed the "Republic of Ireland Act", which severed the last constitutional links with Britain, and the Republic of Ireland was officially inaugurated on Easter

Monday, 1949. Eamon de Valera pointed out that in 1916, they had been fighting for an all-Ireland Republic, and he would take no part in the inaugural ceremonies whatsoever. Shortly thereafter, the English parliament passed the "Ireland Act", which stated that no part of Northern Ireland would ever leave His Majesty's dominion without the approval of the Parliament of Northern Ireland.

The Irish inter-party government of Labour, Fine Gael, and Clann na Poblachta broke up in 1951, following a controversy over free health care for expectant mothers and children, as well as other social issues. There was also another inter-party government from 1954 to 1957. It broke up when Clann na Poblachta withdrew because the government had no clear plan for the unification of Ireland, nor effective economic policies. Fianna Fail again took control in 1957, and in 1959, Eamon de Valera was elected President of Ireland. Sean Lemass, who had fought in the G.P.O. in 1916, became the Taoiseach and under his direction Ireland began a period of rapid economic expansion. In 1965, Sean Lemass traveled to Belfast to meet with the Northern Ireland Prime Minister, Captain Terence O'Neill. This was the first time the two Irish factions had met in negotiations since the early 1920's, and it looked as if the relationship might progress; however, as we all know there was still an extremely rocky road ahead. (Several successive Irish governments, even to this very day, have sought to develop a solution to the problems and provide lasting peace and stability–perhaps soon.)

Ireland at that time also began to look outward and develop relationships within the world community. In 1955, Ireland was admitted to the United Nations and from 1958 onward Irish troops have served in several United Nations' peacekeeping missions. In 1965, Irish soldiers fought for the first time with the United Nations forces. In 1973, Ireland officially became a member of the European Economic Community.

Modern Ireland

World War II had somewhat further alienated the Republic of Ireland from Northern Ireland. The Republic had remained neutral during the conflict while Northern Ireland had been extensively bombed, as it was considered a member of the Allied Forces. On one day alone, the fourth of May 1941, 204 German planes dropped over 95,000 bombs on the harbor and shipyards of Belfast, virtually destroying both and rendering them totally unusable. England was then forced to utilize the ports and naval yards of Derry (now called Londonderry). Britain had helped build up Northern Ireland's industry to support the war effort; and, following the war helped rebuild where needed. Britain also helped establish and maintain governmental institutions in Northern Ireland.

At the time the Republic of Ireland was founded in 1949, the main goals there seemed to be centered around the formation of the new government and the establishment of associated services, along with the settling of political differences among the various factions. It would be approximately ten years before the first serious economic and industrialization programs could be addressed. Hence, at this time the economic conditions (i.e. Per capita income, Gross National Product, Balance of Trade, etc.) were developing more rapidly in the North. However, their lack of addressing the basic political problems and differences would dramatically devastate their economy on down the road.

Let's discuss briefly some of the major events and factors influencing the evolution of Northern Ireland since its inception in 1921. When King George V of England opened the new Northern Ireland Parliament in June of 1921 he pleaded with all Irishmen to, "pause, to stretch out the hand of forbearance and conciliation, to forgive and forget, and to join in making for the land they love a new era of peace, contentment and concil-iation". Well, apparently not many were listening, as the years of Northern Ireland "home rule" (1921-1972) were marked by incredible violence and tension, as both the majority Unionists and the minority Nationalists resented each other's role in society. The mostly Catholic Nationalists had virtually no role in government and suffered great systematic discrimina-tion in many areas, including voting rights, housing and employment. There were generations of poorer Irish being born, living their entire lives, and dying without ever holding a proper job, and people not only need jobs to support their families, they need jobs to promote hope and dignity. They came to deeply resent what they saw as an unnatural and obtrusive partition of the island; and, the mostly Protestant Unionists took an extremely defensive position swearing to never surrender an inch. The Catholics/Nationalists were also reluctant to support or become a part of the institutions they hoped would not survive.

The initial sectarian violence lasted through 1922, leading to the "Special Powers Acts of 1922–1933. The virtually all-protestant Royal Ulster Constabulary was reinforced with the virtually all-protestant Auxiliaries and the Ulster Special Constabulary. These organizations were violently oppressive to Catholics, leading to deep-rooted hatreds and of course dividing the two factions even further.

Also in 1922, the Unionists abolished proportional representation and redrew several boundaries to insure their continued control of most all the local and statewide political councils. (This is when the Unionists gained control of Derry, as up until this time, Derry had always been controlled by Nationalists.) From then on, the Unionists had no problem maintain-ing a sizeable majority in the Parliament of Northern Ireland at Stormont.

Rioting and sectarian violence heightened again in 1935, when the Northern Ireland government banned all parades and marches (in a sup-posed effort to quell violence), and then lifted the ban in July, allowing the Orange Order to conduct their marches and celebrations.

British financial support of the institutions of Northern Ireland also led to further divisions, with the Protestant/Unionist majority enjoying a substantially higher standard of living as the result of basically the establishment of a British welfare state. The Unionists then became even more defensive, and often oppressive, in an effort to maintain this "favored" status. These actions directly led to a heightened anti-partition campaign by the Irish Republican Army, especially after the establishment of The Republic in 1949. These efforts increased dramatically between the years of 1955 and 1962.

In 1963, Captain Terence O'Neill succeeded Sir Basil Brooke as Prime Minister of Northern Ireland. He was the first Prime Minister having not been directly influenced by the events and circumstances of the early 1920's, and he tried honestly to draw the Catholics into the mainstream of Ulster social and political life. These efforts drew great anger and criticism from the Unionists who feared the rising Catholic population would soon vote Northern Ireland into the Republic of Ireland. His most outspoken opponent was the Reverend Ian Paisley of the rather small "Free Presbyterian Church". Opposition to O'Neill's policies was building even within his own party, and increased dramatically after his 1965 meeting with Sean Lemass, the Taoiseach of the Irish Republic. Catholic Civil Rights movements had been increasing steadily in the 1960's, surely following the patterns set in America, and when a Civil Rights March was banned in Derry in October 1968, leading to violence throughout the city, O'Neill was heavily criticized and forced to resign early in 1969.

His successor, Major James Chichester-Clark, was no more successful in stopping the violence. In August 1969, a parade organized by the Orange Order and commemorating the defense of Derry against James II in the year 1690, was attacked by Irish Nationalists. This was followed by virtual all-out warfare in the area of the Catholic Bogside. This led to violence elsewhere in Northern Ireland and eventually the British Army was brought in to restore calm. Following the British government's advise, the government of Northern Ireland began instituting minor reforms.

The Irish Republican Army saw this as the ideal time to bring down the Stormont government. The I.R.A.'s power and influence had increased substantially as they had acted as the defenders of the Nationalist neighborhoods, especially in Belfast and Derry. They had become ever-increasingly more hostile to the British forces, and established "no go" areas in Belfast and Derry, in which the police and British forces were not permitted to enter. Just as their power and ideals were being recognized, philosophical differences led to a division within the I.R.A. The "Official I.R.A.", which was based on the Marxist ideologies of socialized control, broke away from the "Provisional I.R.A." which was more traditional and based on the Revolution of 1916. Both factions continued the fight against partition and British military occupation, and Chichester-Clark resigned in 1971, when the British government refused to step up their attacks on the I.R.A. (Note: Today there are several splinter factions calling themselves I.R.A., many are basically self-proclaiming groups attempting to perpetuate their particular views and/or strategies.)

In March 1972, the British government did in fact suspend the Stormont parliament and government. This was originally to be for one year and the hopes were that, with the Unionists out of power, the battle-weary Nationalists would turn to measures of conciliation and turn away from the I.R.A. However, the backlash from angry Protestants, who now distrusted the British government and became even more militant and violent, only strengthened the position of the I.R.A.

In 1973, the British government proposed a new "Northern Ireland Assembly", in which Catholics and Protestants would share governmental powers that were somewhat more limited than the powers enjoyed by the Stormont government. Elections were held on 28 June 1973, based on proportional representation, and a coalition government was organized at Sunningdale, England, in December of 1973, and was to be called the "Council of Ireland". It took office on 1 January 1974, and from the beginning was undermined by the Unionists who saw it as an attempt to unify Northern Ireland with the Republic. This coalition government collapsed in the face of a Protestant workers' strike in May of that year. In 1976, the Unionists proposed a "Constitutional Convention", basically an effort to assure their continued privileged status, but it found rejection from both the British and the Irish governments immediately.

Levels of violence and conflict fluctuated over the next several years. The Northern Ireland police force (the Royal Ulster Constabulary) was strengthened and every time they would attempt to exert an increased authority, it would bring reprisals from the Irish Republican Army. Since the late 1970's, the British have attempted to steadily diminish the roles of both their military and their political influence. Internment, the holding of suspected members of the I.R.A. without trial and/or the trial without jury for suspected terrorist offenses, which was introduced in 1971, ended in 1975.

Irish Republican prisoners began calling world attention to the situation beginning in the late seventies, by demanding status as "political prisoners". They employed many tactics, but gained world recognition through their "hunger strikes". In 1981, ten prisoners died during a hunger strike, including Bobby Sands, who, while imprisoned and dying, was elected to the British parliament at Westminster, as a representative from the Counties of Fermanagh and South Tyrone.

The Hunger Strike is an ancient Celtic method of fighting injustices. It was codified in the early Celtic Brehon Laws and could be employed as a solution for solving both personal and social wrongdoings. The law provided that if someone was intentionally done wrong by another, he would publicly state the fact and then present himself on the perpetrator's doorstep and begin the fasting. This would hopefully shame, or scare, the perpetrator into righting the wrong. If the plaintiff starved to death, the one responsible had to pay great indemnities to the dead man's family and support them for the remainder of their lives. It was also believed the perpetrator would be subjected to horrific supernatural penalties. This process in Irish is known as "Toscad".

Twenty-two Irish Martyrs have died since 1917, as a result of "Toscad Poblachta" (Political or Republican Hunger Strikes), initiated to call attention to British oppression. These are (from earliest to most recent) Thomas Ashe, Michael Fitzgerald, Joseph Murphy, Terrence MacSwiney (who was the Lord Mayor of Cork), Joseph Whitty, Denis Barry, Andy Sullivan, Tony D'Arcy, Sean McNeela, Sean McCaughey, Michael Gaughan, Frank Stagg, Bobby Sands, Francis Hughes, Ray McCreesh, Patsy O'Hara, Joe McDonnell, Martin Hurson, Kevin Lynch, Kieran Doherty, Tom McElwee, and Michael Devine. (Metress, 1983)

In 1985, the Anglo-Irish Agreement was another effort to provide Northern Ireland with a National Constitution. The Republic of Ireland agreed to be available for consultation, triggering a violent and angry reaction from the Unionist Party and Ian Paisley's Democratic Unionist Party, claiming this was just another attempt at unification of the North and the Republic.

In 1998, on Good Friday, the Belfast Agreement was devised to eventually lead again to Northern Ireland "Home Rule". In May 1999, the Agreement received the approval of the Irish people in simultaneous referendums held in both the Republic and Northern Ireland. Powers were to be devolved by Britain and shared by a cabinet comprised of members from the four largest political parties (two Nationalist, the Social Democratic and Labour Party and the Sinn Fein Party; and, two Unionist, the Ulster Unionist Party and the Democratic Unionist Party), but once again the extremists have employed virtually every technique possible, from fear tactics to boycotts, in an effort to delay, or in reality prevent implementation of the Belfast Agreement. The Northern Ireland power-sharing Assembly was seated in early 2000, but was suspended when the Unionists withdrew their support and participants. As of late 2001, this has happened on at least three separate occasions.

Despite all the subversive efforts, the Peace Process moves forward and it is inevitable that the truthful will of the people will eventually prevail in Northern Ireland, as it should in all other parts of the world. What will it take for this to be accomplished? It will take, as is presently happening, all of the brave men and women within Ireland to step forward, put the past behind them, and make a concerted effort to work for a better future world; and, identify and hold responsible the groups of "thugs" who continue to undermine the Peace Process.

George Mitchell, briefly mentioned previously, spent years working on the Northern Ireland peace negotiations and actually drafted the very first rendering of the Belfast Agreement (also known as the Good Friday Agreement). He delivered a speech in September 2001 at St. Bartholomew's Center for Religious Inquiry in New York, outlining many important points regarding the situation in Northern Ireland. He first pointed out that the cooperative efforts between the concerned governments (primarily Britain and the Republic of Ireland), as well as among the local politicians, have been outstanding in spite of what is often reported. He also noted that they are under extreme pressures from certain elements wanting to undermine the peace process, and that it will most likely take an entirely new generation of leaders working towards peace from the onset to dramatically move forward and attempt to put past animosities behind; and, this leadership is most important and essential to instill the wide spread social belief in peace.

Senator Mitchell further stated that he believed that peace is now imminent in Northern Ireland, as the vast majority on both sides does not wish to return to conflict, even though they may strongly want the negotiations to end on favorable terms for their position. Hope further lies in the fact that the entire island consists of intelligent, well informed, honest, friendly, and loving people with one of the world's highest literacy rates, much higher even than that of the United States. Many are beginning to work together, disregarding their differences, in an effort to promote good, as is evidenced by the new political party, the Northern Ireland Women's Coalition Party, which is comprised of mothers on both sides attempting to secure a better world for their children. (Note: At the present 98% of the children of Northern Ireland attend religiously segregated schools, and never even meet those from the other side, at least until their school years are completed. In an atmosphere such as this it is apparent that stereotypes and mistrust would abound. Those not wanting the peace process to be successful exploit these fears and stereotypes.)

Senator Mitchell concluded by outlining the three relatively minor issues yet to be resolved, the decommissioning of weapons by all paramilitary groups, the demilitarization of Northern Ireland, and the restructuring of the Northern Ireland Police Force; and, by stating that all conflicts can be resolved by men as they were begun by men, and that we must never submit to men of violence.

This certainly won't be easy. The pains of history run very deep, and surely everyone must overcome deeply imbedded feelings of mistrust, and even hatred, to reach a place of acceptance and peace. Perhaps we must contemplate and understand by asking such philosophical questions as, what is the true manner of much of mankind? Could it be that throughout history the peaceful, kind, loving, and gentle people have been mostly annihilated and wiped out by the aggressive and violent elements? What is the nature of many of these humans that have evolved? What is the true nature of these problems we must resolve?

The world is moving forward at an astounding pace with unlimited opportunities for advancement presenting possibilities daily. Ireland has become a world leader in the areas of computer and information technology. The future prospects and benefits in these areas can hardly be yet imagined. It is vitally important to grasp these positive possibilities the future holds and put past evils and animosities at rest behind.

Early in 2001, Pope John Paul II elevated the Irish Archbishop, Desmond Connell, to the College of Cardinals, and one of his very first actions was to gather all the various religious elements of Ireland together in conference at Christ Church Cathedral in Dublin, in an effort to promote unity in Ireland. It was attended by representatives of the Greek Orthodox Church, the Methodist Church, the Lutheran Church, the Catholic Church, the Church of Ireland, and others, with Cardinal

Connell stating that one of his main priorities was to bring all these factions together in an effort to promote discourse and understanding. This is one very important step.

It also leads to another discussion centered on the importance, or relevancy, of our own spiritual beliefs as they relate to our contemplation of ourselves, and our approach to those around us. Catholics and Protestants (as well as Muslims, Jews, Hindus and Buddhists) are taught to Love, Be Compassionate, Honest, and Forgiving of those who persecute you. These are important concepts. They allow you the spiritual power to rise above, and have great influence over, those around you. It takes a special kind of man or woman to step forward; but, when they do, they bring honor to all about them. This "Honor", based on Truth, was seen by our ancient Irish ancestors as being the essence of all life, and should in fact be our guiding hope and foundation for a more positive future existence.

Appendix I

Important Dates In Irish History:

c. 8000 B.C.E.   —Earliest Inhabitants

c. 3700 B.C.E.   —First Neolithic Peoples Arrived

c. 2000 B.C.E.   —Gold Discovered in Wicklow Mountains
Bronze Age peoples flourish–build many stone
tombs

c. 1100 B.C.E.   —First Celtic Tribes Arrived–The Milesians and Gaels

100 C.E.   —Ptolemy writes about Ireland

432   —St. Patrick returned to Ireland as Bishop

c. 485   —St. Brendan "The Navigator" Born

521   —Colm Cille (St. Columba) Born

550–650   —Irish Monasticism flourishes

563   —Iona is founded by St. Columba

590   —Columbanus carries mission to the continent

597   —Death of Colm Cille

700–800   —Christian-Gaelic "Golden Age" (Book of Kells)

794   —Norse (Vikings) First Come to Ireland

837   —Norse Found Dublin

847   —Danes Invade Ireland

914   —Danes Burn Clonmacnoise

941   —Brian Boru Born

1004   —Brian Boru Became High King of Ireland

1014   —Battle of Clontarf—Irish Victory over Norsemen
           Brian Boru is killed

1101   —King O'Brien grants Cashel to the church

1142   —First Cistercian Monastery at Millifont

1170   —Arrival of Earl of Pembroke (Strongbow)

1171   —King Henry II, Norman King of England Invaded
           Ireland

1318   —Battle of Dysert O'Dea

1366   —Kilkenny Statutes written

1509   —Accession of Henry VIII to throne of England

1513   —Gerait Og "Ninth Earl of Kildare" Appt. Lord
            Deputy by Henry VIII

1558   —Death of Queen Mary–Accession of Elizabeth I

1592   —Queen Elizabeth I founded Trinity College

1601   —Battle of Kinsale

1603   —Queen Elizabeth died. James VI of Scotland became
            James I of Engl.

1607   —"Flight of the Earls"
            Ulster Plantation formulated by King James I

1633   —Thomas Wentworth Becomes Governor of Ireland

1641   —The Rising of 1641

1642   —English Civil War

1649   —English Parliament Victorious. Oliver Cromwell sent
            to Ireland

1652-1654   —Ireland and Scotland Defeated. "Great Britain"
            formed

1658   —Cromwell Died.

1685   —Catholic James II Became King of England

1688	—Glorious Revolution. James II fled to Ireland
1690	—Battle of the Boyne River. James II vs. William of Orange.
1691	—Treaty of Limerick
1695	—First "Penal Laws" enacted
1791	—Society of United Irishmen formed by Theobald Wolfe Tone
1795	—"Orange Order" and "The Defenders" organized
1798	—Rising of 1798 (Wexford Rising) Wolfe Tone arrested and sentenced to death
1800	—Act of Union passed (enacted 1 January, 1801)
1823	—Daniel O'Connell forms Catholic Association
1829	—Catholic Emancipation–Catholics could take seats in Parliament
1837	—Accession of Queen Victoria to English throne
1840	—Daniel O'Connell organizes Repeal Association
1842	—Young Irelanders publish first issue of "The Nation"
1845	—Blight of potato crop is beginning of Great Famine

1846	—Corn Laws Repealed
1848-1849	—Worst years of famine–over one million die
1858	—James Stephens founds Irish Republican Brotherhood. Fenian Brotherhood founded in America
1863	—" The Irish People" newspaper founded
1865	—William Butler Yeats born
1867	—Disestablishment of Church of Ireland
1873	—Home Rule League formed
1875	—Charles Stewart Parnell elected MP from County Meath
1884	—Gaelic Athletic Association founded
1886	—First Home Rule Bill introduced by Gladstone
1890	—National Museum of Ireland founded
1891	—Second Home Rule Bill introduced Formation of The Gaelic League (Conradh na Gaelige)
1892	—National Literary Society formed by W.B. Yeats and Douglas Hyde

1896   —James Connolly forms Irish Republican Socialist Party

1899   —"United Irishman" newspaper founded by Arthur Griffith

1900   —Cumann na nGaedhael Party formed by Arthur Griffith

1903   —Abbey Theatre formed by W.B. Yeats and Lady Gregory

1905   —Sinn Fein founded

1909   —Land Purchase Act introduced

1912   —Third Home Rule Bill introduced and passed by House of Commons

1913   —Ulster Volunteer Force established Irish Citizen Army and Irish National Volunteers formed

1914   —Home Rule Act passed, but suspended due to WW I

1916   —Easter Rising in Dublin followed by executions

1917   —Sinn Fein party defeats Parliamentary party in Irish elections

1919   —Dail Eireann meets in Dublin

1919-1921   —Irish War of Independence

1920   —First Black and Tans arrive—"Bloody Sunday"

1921	—Anglo-Irish Treaty providing for Irish Free State and Northern Ireland
1922-1923	—Irish Civil War
1926	—Eamon de Valera leaves Sinn Fein and forms Fianna Fail
1933	—Fine Gael party formed
1937	—Constitution of Eire– Articles 2 and 3 lay claim also to the Six Counties
1939	—WW II Begins, Eire declares neutrality Death of W. B. Yeats
1941	—German air raids in Derry and Belfast
1945	—WW II ends
1949	—Republic of Eire (Ireland) founded
1966	—Anglo-Irish Free Trade Agreement Ulster Volunteer Force outlawed
1968	—Civil Rights marches begin in Belfast and Derry
1970	—Social Democratic and Labour Party founded I.R.A. splits into "Provisionals" and "Officials"
1971	—Britain agrees to Northern Ireland Internment-1576 people interned Democratic Unionist Party founded by Ian Paisley

1972	—"Bloody Sunday" in Derry. Direct Rule imposed by Britain
1973	—Republic of Ireland and U.K. join European Economic Community
1975	—Northern Ireland Convention convened. Internment suspended
1976	—British Ambassador killed in Dublin
1979	—Earl Mountbatten killed in County Sligo
1981	—Death of Bobby Sands and nine other hunger strikers at Long Kesh
1985	—Anglo-Irish Agreement
1990	—IRA bombing of London Stock Exchange
1991	—IRA mortar bombing of 10 Downing Street
1994	—First IRA ceasefire
1998	—Belfast Agreement (Good Friday Agreement)
1999	—People in both Republic of Ireland and Northern Ireland approve Belfast Agreement in referendums
2000	—Power-sharing Northern Ireland Assembly established

Appendix II

Republic of Ireland Population by Provinces and Counties:

Province	County	Population
Leinster		1,860,037
	Carlow	40,946
	Dublin	1,024,429
	Kildare	122,516
	Kilkenny	73,613
	Laois	52,325
	Longford	30,293
	Louth	90.707
	Meath	105,540
	Offaly	58,448
	Westmeath	61,882
	Wexford	102,045
	Wicklow	97,293
Munster		1,008,443
	Clare	90,826
	Cork	409,814
	Kerry	121,719
	Limerick	161,856
	Tipperary	132,620
	Waterford	91,608

Connacht		422,909
	Galway	180,304
	Leitrim	25,297
	Mayo	110,696
	Roscommon	51,876
	Sligo	54,736
Ulster (portion of)		232,012
	Cavan	52,756
	Donegal	127,994
	Monaghan	51,262

*Taken from 1991 Census (Department of Foreign Affairs, 1995. Note–Figures are sure to be higher as there has been a substantial migration into The Republic of Ireland since the later half of the 1990's.

References/Further Reading:

Adams, Gerry Free Ireland: Towards a Lasting Peace. Roberts Rinehart Publishers, Niwot, Colorado. 1994.

Asplin, P. W. A. Medieval Ireland c.1170-1495: A Bibliography of Secondary Works. Royal Irish Academy, Dublin. 1971.

Cahill, Thomas How the Irish Saved Civilization: The Untold Story of Ireland's Heroic Role from the Fall of Rome To the Rise of Medieval Europe. Doubleday, New York. 1995.

Department of Foreign Affairs Facts About Ireland. Government of Ireland, Dublin. 1995.
Duffy, Kevin Who Were the Celts? Barnes and Noble Books, New York. 1996.

Duncan, Anthony The Elements of Celtic Christianity. Element Books Limited, Shaftesbury, Dorset. 1992.

Dunne, John J. Shrines Of Ireland. Veritas Publications, Dublin. 1989.

Foster, Robert Fitzroy (ed.) The Oxford Illustrated History of Ireland. Oxford University Press, Oxford. 1989.

Hyde, Douglas A Literary History of Ireland. London. 1899.

Kenny, Michael The Fenians. The National Museum of Ireland, Dublin. 1994.

Mac Annaidh, Seamas Irish History. Parragon Books, Bath, UK. 2001.

Maclean, Magnus The Literature of the Celts. Blackie and Son Ltd., London. 1902.

MacManus, Seumas The Story of the Irish Race. Random House, New York. 1990

McCormack, W. J. Ascendancy and Tradition in Anglo-Irish Literary History from 1789 to 1939. Oxford University Press, Oxford. 1985.

Metress, Seamus The Hunger Strike and the Final Struggle. Connolly Books, Detroit. 1983.

Monk, Michael A. and John Sheehan (ed.) Early Medieval Munster Archaeology, History and Society. Cork University Press, Cork. 1998.
Murphy, Gerard The Ossianic Lore and Romantic Tales of Medieval Ireland. Cultural Relations Committee, Dublin. 1955.

O'Brien, Maire and Conor Cruise A Concise History of Ireland. Beekman House, New York. 1972.

O'Ferrall, Fergus Catholic Emancipation: Daniel O'Connell and the Birth of Irish Democracy. Dublin. 1985.

Piehler, H. A. Ireland For Everyman. W. W. Norton and Company, New York. 1961.

Pollard, H. B. C. The Secret Societies of Ireland: Their Rise and Progress. The Irish Historical Press, Kilkenny. 1998.

Reeves-Smyth, Terence and Fred Hammond Landscape Archaeology In Ireland. British Archaeology Reports, Oxford. 1983.

Rodgers, Michael and Marcus Losack Glendalough: A Celtic Pilgrimage. The Columba Press, Dublin. 1998.

Ryan, Meda The Day Michael Collins Was Shot. Poolbeg Press Ltd., Dublin. 1989.

Ryan, Michael Ireland and Insular Art: A.D. 500-1200. Royal Irish Academy, Dublin. 1985.

Rynne, Etienne The Art of Early Irish Illumination. The Capuchin Annual, Vol. 36. 1969.

_____ The Revival of Irish Art in the Late 19th and Early 20th Century. In: Themes In Irish Culture, Topic 24, Washington and Jefferson College, Washington, Pa. 1972.

Saint Benedict A Rule for Beginners. Order of Saint Benedict, Collegeville, Minn. 1981.

Sawyer, Peter Kings and Vikings: Scandanavia and Europe AD 700-1100. London. 1982.

Scherman, Katharine The Flowering of Ireland: Saints, Scholars, And Kings. Barnes and Noble Books, New York. 1996.

Simms, J. G. Jacobite Ireland 1685-1691. London. 1969.

Thomson, David and Moyra McGusty (eds.) The Irish Journals of Elizabeth Smith 1840-1850. Oxford University Press, Oxford. 1980.

Wall, Maureen The Penal Laws. Irish Royal Historical Society, Dublin. 1961.

Wallace, Martin A Short History of Ireland. Barnes and Noble Books, New York. 1996.

Whitelock, Dorothy and Rosamond McKitterick and David Dumville (eds.) Ireland In Early Medieval Europe. Cambridge University Press, Cambridge. 1982.

Yeats, William Butler (ed.) Fairy and Folk Tales of Ireland. Colin Smythe Gerrards Cross, Buckinghamshire. 1973.

About the Author

Dennis Sommers is the Director of the Institute of Irish History and Culture, located at Trinity College, Dublin. He holds a Doctorate degree in Theology, is interested in Irish Monastic History, conducts an International Summer School at Trinity, and greatly appreciates your input and correspondence at *www.instituteofirishculture@ireland.com*